A Ragged Mountain Press
WOMAN'S GUIDE

SNOWBOARDING

JULIA CARLSON

Series Editor, Molly Mulhern Gross

Camden, Maine • New York • San Francisco • Washington, D.C. • Auckland
Bogotá • Caracas • Lisbon • London • Madrid • Mexico City • Milan
Montreal • New Delhi • San Juan • Singapore • Sydney • Tokyo • Toronto

McGraw Hill

Look for these other Ragged Mountain Press Woman's Guides

Sea Kayaking, Shelley Johnson
Backpacking, Adrienne Hall
Mountaineering, Andrea Gabbard
Fly Fishing, Dana Rikimaru

Sailing, Doris Colgate
Canoeing, Laurie Gullion
Skiing, Maggie Loring
Winter Sports, Iseult Devlin

Ragged Mountain Press

A Division of The McGraw-Hill Companies

10 9 8 7 6 5 4 3 2 1

Copyright © 1999 by Julia Carlson

All rights reserved. The publisher takes no responsibility for the use of any of the materials or methods described in this book, nor for the products thereof. The name "Ragged Mountain Press" and the Ragged Mountain Press logo are trademarks of The McGraw-Hill Companies. Printed in the United States of America.

Library of Congress Cataloging-in-Publication Data
Carlson, Julia, 1968–
    Snowboarding/Julia Carlson.
        p. cm.—(A Ragged Mountain Press woman's guide)
    Includes bibliographical references (p. 134) and index.
    ISBN 0-07-012038-2 (alk. paper)
    1. Snowboarding. 2. Outdoor recreation for women. I. Title.
    II. Series.
GV857.S57C37 1999
796.9—dc21   ·
                            98-41572
                            CIP

Questions regarding the content of this book should be addressed to:
  Ragged Mountain Press
  P.O. Box 220, Camden, ME 04843
  www.raggedmountainpress.com

Questions regarding the ordering of this book should be addressed to:
  The McGraw-Hill Companies
  Customer Service Department
  P.O. Box 547, Blacklick, OH 43004
  Retail customers: 1-800-262-4729
  Bookstores: 1-800-722-4726

Printed by Quebecor Printing Company, Fairfield, PA
Edited by Jerry Novesky
Design by Carol Inouye, Inkstone Communications Design
Project management by Janet Robbins
Page layout and production assistance by Shannon Thomas
Illustrations by Elayne Sears
Art editing by Cia Boynton
Photos by Dennis Curran/Sports File, unless otherwise noted

• •

"I'm on chairlift #8 at Mount Snow in Vermont, a borrowed snowboard dangling from my left foot, the bright April sun's warmth helping me temporarily forget my sore, wet body. I look over to my companion on the lift and see smiling back at me a scrappy twelve-year-old boy. 'Rad sticker,' he declares, looking at my newly placed "Ride Like A Girl" sticker. He smiles approval. For a moment I forget my age, my gender, my responsibilities. I wonder how I appear to this kid. My blonde hair stuffed in under a hat, my face hidden under Oakleys, my body disguised by my baggy coat and pants. I could be any age, any gender. But I'm not. Here I am, a 29-year-old woman who, after only three days, is ready to trade in her world for the flight on the board. I am, as they say, stoked to be here."

—Amy Speace, singer, songwriter
from New York City

• •

Foreword

"**Y**ou want me to do *what?*"

"Ride the chair."

"I'm not ready."

"Yes you are."

With those words of blunt encouragement, my snowboard instructor headed over to the chairlift. I hobbled behind, snowboard awkwardly attached to one foot, looking surreptitiously up the steep hill. This particular ski area (one I am blessed with having almost in my backyard) is sadly lacking any "bunny slope." I knew that even if I negotiated the lift—more about that in a moment—there was no way I could make it down the run without spending more time *in* the snow than on top of it. I desperately wanted to head in the other direction, claiming tiredness or ill-fitting gear (and I certainly had a good excuse, since my feet, crammed into boys' boots, were killing me). But I was paying for the lesson and I had only been at it for 20 or 30 minutes . . . so off I went.

Luckily the line for the chairlift was short, and I saw no one nearby that I knew, yet the sight of that small ramp leading down to the loading area, and the knowledge that an equally small exit ramp waited at the top of the lift, petrified me. Somehow, I did that clunky one-foot snowboard walk down the ramp (the instructor had breezed over this walking-with-snowboard part, and I really wasn't feeling very secure with it: see pages 39–41 for Julia's excellent description). I turned to catch the chair just in time and managed to sit on the lift, rising into the air without mishap. My landing at the top was graceless, but I delayed falling until I was off the ramp, so I took no casualties with me. And you know what? I felt great! I had done it, the very thing that had petrified me most about taking a snowboard lesson!

And the trip down? Well, it wasn't speedy, and no, I never did link a turn (I was busy working on my "falling leaf" exercise, see pages 51–52), but like the chairlift ride, that trip—and the instructor's confidence in me—had shown me that I really could handle the terrain.

I didn't have the benefit of *Snowboarding: A Woman's Guide* when I took that first lesson, but I sure wish I had. First off I would have known better how to approach the lift line (see pages 41–42), and I would have had Julia's great advice about riding the chair (see page 42 for the three Ps). It was precisely because I couldn't find a book like the one you're holding that we set out to create The Ragged Mountain Press Woman's Guides. I was desperately looking for books and articles that addressed my concerns as an outdoorswoman. How should I have selected an instructor to make that first lesson a success? Rental shops are flooded with all kinds of gear and equipment: What are the right questions to ask when you want to rent a beginner's snowboard outfit? Do I really need to live with misfitting boys' boots or are there finally women's boots? (See page 27 for a great discussion of making sure you try the sport with the right "borrowed" equipment.)

Snowboarding: A Woman's Guide answers those questions, providing instruction and advice I wish I'd had before heading onto that slope with aching feet and a humungous fear of riding the chair. Here you'll find other women's snowboarding experiences told in a manner that respects how women learn and grow.

What's so different about the way women learn? If you're like me, you want to hear a description of a move or tactic before launching into it. I'm a fan of the talk-it-over-and-think-it-through-first school of outdoor learning. I prefer to ask questions *before* I'm asked to get on a chairlift, petrified that I won't be able to get off at the top. I want to hear advice from someone like me, someone I know and trust. And I like to learn in a group so I can hear other folks' questions—and know I'm not the only one wondering whether I'm a goofy or a regular rider (see page 29).

We've done our best to mimic the learning conditions of a woman's instructional clinic in The Ragged Mountain Press Woman's Guides. Here you'll find lots of women's voices: your instructor's, of course, but also voices of women from all walks who love the outdoors. *Snowboarding: A Woman's Guide* provides solutions, advice, and stories from women who have done what you are about to do: learn to snowboard. I hope Julia's words and approach help get you out riding and enjoying, by yourself or with a friend. I'll look for you out there.

Between snowboarding days, drop us a note to tell us how we're doing and how we can improve these guides to best suit you and your learning style.

MOLLY MULHERN GROSS
Series Editor, The Ragged Mountain Press Woman's Guides
Camden, Maine
October 1998

An avid outdoorswoman, Molly Mulhern Gross enjoys running, hiking, camping, sea kayaking, telemark skiing, in-line skating, and biking and has just started snowboarding. She is Director of Editing, Design, and Production at Ragged Mountain Press and International Marine.

CONTENTS

CONTENTS

Acknowledgments

This book is the work of many people, mostly women, whom you will meet in its pages. The intent is not to be Julia Carlson Goes Off On Snowboarding, but various women of the industry (and a couple of quality guys) offering up their collective wisdom about the sport that has become so important to all of us.

In addition to the pros and experts, there are plenty of appearances by newcomers, old farts and lots of other Real Live Snowboarding Women. I can't mention everyone here, so thanks to all for their contributions. Super special personal props go to the following:

Molly Mulhern Gross, badass and editor of The Ragged Mountain Press Woman's Guides, who made this series happen and hired me to do the snowboard book.

Janet Robbins and **Shannon Thomas** of Ragged Mountain Press: For layout wizardry above and beyond the call, and for their patience and humor in dealing with my requests.

Betsy Shaw, world-champion snowboarder and first-rate travel buddy: For being the star of the instructional sequences, which in my view made the book; and for making it entertaining (as usual).

Ali Napolitano, friend and snowboard industry vet: For hours of reading and insightful commentary, for being the woman who coined the phrase "Ride Like A Girl," (and for the righteous strawberry shortcake).

Greta Brumbach, research and testing engineer at Ride Snowboards: For adding her years of product development experience to the equipment section and for being the only other full-fledged tech betty I know of.

Katie Bush and the campers of **Women Only Snowboard Camps:** For providing many laughs and feedback on what really works.

Patty Segovia, So Cal skate queen and photographer: For shooting women with incredible style and supporting this project with hundreds of photos.

Jules Older, professor of a class called Writing for Real at the University of Vermont: For the novel conviction that art for money is still art. (It was impossible to ace his class unless we actually sold something. Revolutionary!)

Johnny Gerndt, testing coordinator at Burton Snowboards: A belated thank-you for several years of toys, answers, references and generally being a friend when it counts.

Jong, Geronimo, Skippy, and **Captain Mike:** For the quality entertainment.

And of course **Dad, Mom, Jim** and **Kitty:** For making me lucky to have four parents.

Best to all & enjoy.
Julia C.
Stowe, Vermont, October 1998

Chapter 1

WHY RIDE?

Photo by Patty Segovia; Rider: Stine Brun Kjeldas

Anticipation had us up early on the first day of vacation, with bluebird skies, fresh snow, and a pile of new toys waiting under the Christmas tree. It looked like a good year, with brand-new gear for everyone in the family. At the top of the heap were the cutting edge for 1988—two pairs of the hot new "ladies'" skis, one each for me and for my father's long-time girlfriend, Kitty.

It had all the makings of a perfect day, except the boards turned out to be as soft as noodles. Even with 18 years of experience and a couple of ski instructors for parents, I wound up doing somersaults down all my favorite trails. Kitty wasn't experiencing any quantum leaps in skill either, so we cracked jokes about being out of shape and confined ourselves to gentler terrain for a while.

Of course, what we really needed was a change of equipment. Kitty still says she was out of shape and needed lessons, but she did do some careful shopping, bought better boards, and noticed a big difference. With less patience and more confidence, I eyed snowboarding. One of my best friends was getting really good at it, and suddenly the vision of fluid turns, deep carves, and fun little tricks was stuck in my mind. Tempting. I hesitated a few days (probably more chicken to abandon my "expert" skier status than anything else), but what the heck, those cheesy skis were no fun anyway, and my brother was ready to copilot.

So we rented boards for New Year's. I'll admit it was awkward at first—facing sideways instead of down the mountain and learning to balance over the edges with my toes and heels—

but there we were, just a few hours later, linking turns together under a forgotten chair lift in six inches of fresh powder. I'll never forget the sensation.

Too bad it's tough to describe without gushing foolishly. (I used to say it's like lightning in your bones, but they quoted me in the paper and now I'll never live it down.) So I'll try the details: the physical exhilaration of turning the board in a hundred slightly different ways; the energizing effect of being high on a mountain with trails stretching out in every direction like so many invitations; the way every detail—every bump, dip, chute, flat spot—is an opportunity for fun when you're standing on a snowboard. Nothing in my experience offers quite the same mix of freedom, simplicity, and full-on entertainment.

A friend of a friend had a board for sale back home, which I bought as soon as I could scrape together the cash. Soon your basic, over-achieving college student was scheduling classes around hill time and postponing that fancy post-graduation job for a snowboarding "year off" in Colorado—which turned into four years of pro riding, then four more coaching, writing, and designing next year's toys for the world's leading snowboard manufacturer. And so on, until today, when I should probably be considering rehab.

Except I'm not alone. A 1996 National Snowboarder Survey by the SnowSports Industries America (SIA) indicates snowboarders are a pretty dedicated bunch: We're usually the first to be there when the lifts open up for the season and often are the last to put our boards away in the spring; we ride an average of 20 days each winter (twice as often as the average skier) and have a habit of bringing a bunch of friends. They've even called us "evangelists . . . one of the primary reasons that snowboarding continues to grow." The sport is catching on so fast these days that in June 1997, *Transworld Snowboarding Business* declared it "the fastest growing sport in the United States."

So, what's all the fuss about? Rest assured, behind all the hype is a virtual buffet of good reasons to get fired up about snowboarding. Help yourself.

THE TOP 10 REASONS WHY SNOWBOARDING RULES

1. **It's easy to learn.** You don't have to be skinny, strong, or 17 years old (though it may help you feel more of each), and most people can connect turns in a day. Stacey Andrus is 29 and hesitated to try it for months, but once she did, she surprised herself by learning to turn both ways in less than two hours. Then there's Millie Merrill, a 50-something CEO of her own company, lifelong skier, and natural athlete—she nailed it in one run, despite ridiculously inappropriate rental equipment. Sure, there are moments of frustration (including a few on your derriere), but those are easily minimized and more than offset by flashes of inspiration and progress. Stacey, who had been so hesitant at first, couldn't stop grinning once she got out there. "I can't believe how fun this is," she kept saying. "It's so much easier than I thought it would be."

"**T**he learning stages of snow-boarding flow so smoothly that I can distinctly remember seeing improvements in my riding with each run I took. Feeling these positive changes is very satisfying and this constant gratification is where the addiction lies. It makes you want to keep playing until it gets dark, just like when we were kids. Then there is the sensation of the pure, unadulterated carve. The thrill of making a clean, efficient turn

Betsy Shaw, 1995 World Giant Slalom Champion and member of the 1998 Olympic Snowboard team, has spent the last ten years training and racing on hillsides all over the globe. Her world-class technique is featured on the cover (lower left) and in the book's instructional sequences (Chapters 3 and 4).

and using every inch and fiber of the board is beyond description. Even after years of ski racing I never felt a sensation as powerful as this. Being one efficiently dynamic unit is unique to snowboarding: Whereas skiing really only involves the feet and the knees, snowboarding is a full-body experience."

—Betsy Shaw

2. **Once you get started, it's easy to get better.** Take my friend Astrid, for example. Not exactly a jock before she started snowboarding, she took to it in a day. Within weeks she and a girlfriend were turning heads all over the mountain. In a year she moved to Colorado to be an instructor; in two she started racing and was running gates down some of the steepest trails in the Rocky Mountains.

    Then there's Mary McKhann, a badass grandmother who started riding just a few years ago. A big fan of hard boots and alpine boards, she's now a coach for Women Only Snowboard Camps in Sugarbush, Vermont, where she spends winter weekends teaching other women to carve all over the hill.

    It helps to live near the mountains (as Mary and Astrid do) so you can practice

all the time, but even weekend warriors like singer/songwriter Amy Speace, who must drive from New York City to the mountains every time she wants to ride, can cover most of the mountain with style within a season.

3.   **You'll never get bored.** Like Millie or Amy, you can start off on a silly rental setup or someone else's old beater that really doesn't fit quite right and still have the time of your life. Then, when the bug bites really hard, you can whip out the plastic for a custom setup and blow yourself away with the quantum leaps you make on the hill.

But it doesn't stop there. Even when the learning curve flattens a bit and you start to wonder about having exhausted the possibilities, there are whole new worlds of fun waiting all over the mountain. On snow days, you can chase fresh powder tracks early in the morning with all the other junkies waiting in line for the first chair. Or, say you've developed a taste for speed: Most mountains use grooming machines that leave trails of fresh corduroy ripe for poaching first thing in the morning. Show up early and it's just like having a highway all to yourself—there's plenty of room to go as fast as you dare (and no need to worry about being polite).

Or maybe speed doesn't sound that appetizing (yet), but you have noticed all those kids boosting airs in the park, and discovered a growing desire to sneak in for a try when nobody's looking. Mornings are key in this instance as well. The snow may be a bit harder (that's why all the regulars are still in bed), but you get all the time and room you need to reach for that first moment of weightlessness. Pretty soon you're an adrenaline slave, hiking way past pooped in search of bigger air and new tricks.

Sound unlikely? "I'm an awesome snowboarder now," Stacey says, anxiously awaiting her second sea-son. "I'll never forget that first day. It was so fun! I went every weekend after that, both days. I do

Bottom photo: Author and former pro rider Julia Carlson demonstrates a grab in the park at Women Only Snowboard Camps. (Photo by Mike Coburn)

Left: Rider Lynn Martel hikes for fresh tracks in the backcountry. **Right:** Never let a snowstorm drive you indoors. Riding in powder might just be the most fun you'll ever have on a snowboard. Riders: Karleen Jeffery, Jennie McDonald, and friends. (Photos by Dan Hudson)

everything now—pipe, park, trees—everything. I even caught my first air. I can't wait to go again."

And that's still just the beginning. Steeps, bumps, chutes, backcountry—each is a separate discipline, yet the thrill is always the same. You can spend 10 years getting the hang of it all and still wind up waiting impatiently for snow to fly in the fall.

4. **The vibe is positive, contagious, and will go to your head.** Snowboarding is still driven by an "alternative" crowd whose lifestyle is comfortable, relaxed, permissive,

• •

"I just can't emphasize enough how it's not about who's better or gets to the bottom first. Nine times out of ten the people you wind up riding with just want to help you learn. They'll help you and push you, but it's not a competition. Skiing is completely different that way—always a competition. Snowboarding seems to be more 'live and let live.' In the pipe, for example, even complete strangers support you. They just know you're there to learn, and respect that. It brings the comfort level up and the intimidation level down, which is so key if you're self-conscious like I am. Out of all the reasons to ride, this is the one that matters to me most. It's really something special about snowboarding that I just don't get in other sports."

—Alison Napolitano, co-founder of Team Betty/Ride Like A Girl™ and former Women's Outerwear Product Manager for Burton Snowboards

• •

and supportive. You feel encouraged to do whatever you want, which can lead to surprising yourself both on the hill and off.

First come the comfortable little risks. Like trading in those stretch pants for hot new snowboard stuff. They may seem loose and less feminine, but suddenly you have freedom of movement that feels so good you could never go back. Why would you want to?

Then you contemplate racing stripes in your hair and that bump run you've been eyeing. Why not? So you put three turns together, then the whole run. You never thought it was possible, but there you are. It feels so good that you seek more challenges, and more. You want to go faster, and try it. Learn to jump, and do it. Now you're a goner. Sell everything; we're moving to the mountains.

5.   **The equipment is easy to manage, and there's great stuff for women.**

Snowboards are like sports cars: high performance in a small package and super fun to drive. The high performance in snowboarding comes mostly from your stance on the board. This is an easy one: It's hard to balance on one foot (that's why we make other people do it, so we can point at each other and laugh, right?). You wouldn't lift a heavy box that way, or even jump out of bed, because you have better balance and twice the strength on two feet. The same goes for sliding down a mountain. On skis you've only got one foot at a time to get you through those turns, while the other practically dangles in mid-air. But stand on a snowboard and you've got both feet on the ground— twice the power, twice the stability, twice the control. You can push your board around, dig your edges into the snow, go full speed ahead, or stop on a dime with total confidence.

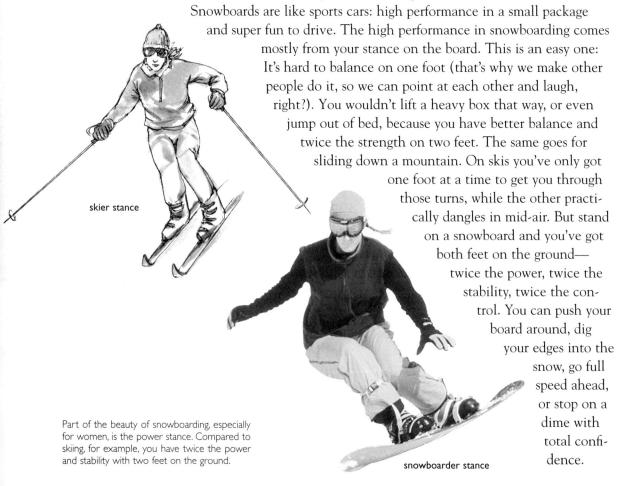

skier stance

snowboarder stance

Part of the beauty of snowboarding, especially for women, is the power stance. Compared to skiing, for example, you have twice the power and stability with two feet on the ground.

The only drawback to a snowboarding stance comes at the very beginning—you have to get the hang of balancing over your edges without that extra foot to put down. But hey, that part doesn't take very long to learn and the payoff just keeps coming.

Another big plus is the shape of the board. Mix a surfboard, a skateboard, and a pair of skis and you've got a 1960s snow-sliding toy called the Snurfer. Then add 20-odd years of experimentation and development, intensified by the rivalry between early snowboard manufacturers like Sims and Burton. Voilà! The modern snow-board, a sophisticated toy with superior handling in a variety of snow conditions. It floats like a surfboard, so you can cruise along in thigh-deep powder or 6 inches of spring mush without getting bogged down; it carves like an alpine ski because it bends and has metal edges, but you can feel the board better with two feet fastened along its length and work it harder with all the might of those two legs. It's also got a curved (or "kick") tail like a skateboard that slides over uneven snow, so you can ride switchstance (backwards) with ease and take off, spin, and land in all different directions.

But that's just the board. I probably don't need to mention how nice it is to have your hands free (no clunky ski poles) so you can do tricks with grabs, clean your goggles, wave to your friends, or just wipe your nose. Or that soft snowboarding boots are lighter and more comfortable than bulky plastic ski boots (plus you can walk and drive in them). Or that snow-board bindings are light, comfortable, and

Bev Sanders, who co-founded Avalanche Snowboards with husband Chris in the late eighties, was one of the first women to get involved in snowboarding on the equipment side. "We never had enough boards to go around," says Bev. "I kept selling them faster than he could make them, so half the time, one of us would wind up skiing." Not now though. These days Avalanche sells the Sanders 148, a board designed just for Bev.

Riders Melissa Longfellow and Bethany Stevens founded *Fresh and Tasty* women's snowboarding magazine in 1994. Named for a box of pancakes, "FAT" inspired three years of loyal support and controversy before changing to web-only format in 1998. (Photo by Gregg Greenwood, courtesy *Fresh and Tasty*)

Pro Rider Michele Taggart looking buff at a summer training session on the glacier at Mt. Hood, Oregon. (Photo by Patty Segovia)

infinitely adjustable, so you can customize your stance, ride in perfect comfort, and do all kinds of tricks with your legs in different positions. You lose a lot of baggage snowboarding. If you're into low maintenance, it's the only way to go.

A final benefit is the recent explosion in equipment designed specifically for women. Not too long ago there weren't many snowboarders around, never mind *women* snowboarders, and women's products weren't much of an issue. We all flailed happily on boards that were literally half a foot too wide and way too long. These days, the opposite is true: Women are snowboarding in record numbers, so shops and manufacturers are scrambling to meet our needs. Walk into any rental or specialty shop and you should find a variety of boards, boots, bindings, and clothing with female-friendly features.

6. **It's good for you.** Snowboarding is the best kind of physical activity: Too much fun to feel like exercise, but still strenuous enough to make you break a sweat. People sometimes doubt its effectiveness (note the chairlift), but the workout is there if you want it. You can charge entire runs all day, making your legs burn and your lungs pump in search of oxygen. Or you can take it easy, cruising along on gentle trails and stopping often to catch your breath. Or you can do both, in whatever combination you please.

Which body parts are we talking about here? As you might expect, riding down a mountain all day will give your quads and hamstrings quite the workout, and your calves do a lot of pushing to get those edges into the snow. But snowboarding also hits some rarely-used muscles in between, like those ad- and abductors on the sides of your upper legs and the little ripples connected to your calves. And let's not forget those all-important glutes, which do indeed get higher and tighter with every run.

Here's another surprise: Snowboarding also works your mid- and upper body. Keeping a firm midsection is essential for transmitting power to your edges, which means those abs get a constant, gentle squeeze. Holding your arms centered in front of you while the rest of your body is in constant motion also requires steady, if seemingly effortless, adjustment.

7. **It's surprisingly safe.** The odds of getting injured while snowboarding are way in your favor. Mary Bozack, the first female member of the Professional Ski Patrol Association and currently the director of ski patrol at Stowe, Vermont, explains, "Of all the people on the mountain—and that means skiers, snowboarders, Telemark skiers and everyone else—national figures suggest about six per thousand will be involved in an accident [per season]." If my math is right, that's a 99.4 percent chance that you're going to be just fine on the slopes.

A second-year snowboarder at the age of 43, Bozack explains that the majority of serious injuries tend to affect teenage boys. "When it comes to women—especially older, more sensible women—I won't go so far as to say it's not going to happen," but it's not exactly a major concern, she says.

The most common snowboarder injuries are to the wrists. As Jan Idzikowski, of High Country Health Care in Vail, Colorado, explains, this is "particularly true for beginners" who haven't learned to balance over their edges yet. A physician's

RIDER PROFILE

SARAH COGHLAN

Age: 24
Height: 5'7"
Weight: 140
Foot Size: 8
Years Riding: 8

KELSEY COGHLAN

Age: 2½
Height: 35 inches
Weight: 27
Foot Size: 7 (toddler)
Years Riding: "Since she was 8 weeks in utero" and "actively since 27 months."

BOARD ◄ - ◄ - - -

"I ride a Burton Supermodel 151 with medium freestyle bindings and size 8 freestyle boots," says Sarah. "I had to move up to a longer board while I was pregnant because I got so much heavier." Kelsey rides a Burton Chopper 95, which is twin-tipped (built to go in either direction), because kids standing out on the hill don't care which end is forward— when they see something they want, like mommy, they just point whichever end of the board is closest and go. *(continued on page 18)*

RIDER PROFILE
CONTINUED

BINDINGS AND BOOTS ◄----------------------------

Kelsey uses Burton size XS freestyle bindings, made with oversize buckles for "parent-free" operation. They are quite large for her feet (as most bindings and boards will be for a few years yet). As for boots, "They don't make snowboard boots small enough for her so she wears her favorite pink Sorels," Sarah says.

ON SNOWBOARDING WHILE PREGNANT ◄---

"I got lots of comments, and I didn't snowboard with my first pregnancy. But with Kelsey I felt that being active was so good for both of us, and I just knew that my body would tell me when to stop. I have friends in the city who were told absolutely not, don't do it, but my doctors gave me the full go ahead—my obstetrician said, "Snowboard until your body tells you to stop.'" Husband Andy, an old-school pro snowboarder himself and now a full-time coach, also was totally supportive of the decision to go ahead and ride.

"I wouldn't do it if you're a beginner—your body goes through enough when you're pregnant—but for me it was easy," Sarah says. "I still feel that snowboarding was one of the best things I did. I just felt really connected to Kelsey when I was riding—that it was something we were doing together, that she could feel the rocking, and that I was taking good care of myself. Andy agreed that it really soothed the baby, and of course we think it's one of the reasons she completely rips now! Once you get big enough, your balance is off and it's hard to keep your weight centered. Then it's too awkward."

As for falling, Sarah is skeptical of the myth that it's dangerous for pregnant women to be active. "Hollywood would have you think that if you fall down, you miscarry. No way! The baby is so cushioned, it would take a lot more than that. I fell once," she confesses. "I was running gates and caught a tip. It hurt my boobs more than anything else, but that was the day I decided to stop."

ON RIDING WITH THE FAMILY ◄---

"I don't get to ride as much as I used to because I'm a full-time mom. Andy and I have three daughters—Kelsey, and Shay and Delaney (9-month-old twins). Andy and I have brought Kelsey to the mountain and she does great. She likes to go really fast and jump. She also loves to go backcountry in the fields behind our house. Snowboarding is a great sport for us as a family because we will all be able to do it together." As a mom, Sarah volunteers, "Snowboarding is one of the more relaxing things I do. It's a great stress release. When I go out and ride, I feel free."

assistant for Dr. Peter Janes, who has researched the subject with 4,500 patients over the last 10 years, he is quick to add that "the use of wrist guards has been proven to reduce the risk of injury by 50 percent." Recalling her own learning experience last season, Mary suggests taking a lesson: "A lot of those wrist injuries come from reaching back to break a fall," she says, whereas "instructors now are teaching people to roll sideways and land on their hip, which for most of us is a somewhat larger surface." She reminds us that the chances of getting hurt on the slopes are actually quite slim. "Just have fun," she says, "I did, and I plan to do a lot more snowboarding this season."

8. **It's cheaper than ever.** The major expenses involved in snowboarding are the equipment and lift tickets, plus lodging and transportation if you don't live close to the slopes. Add them up and, at a glance, the costs may seem prohibitive.

    Take a closer look, however, and it's not that bad: Equipment is cheaper than it has ever been, and there are plenty of ways to cut corners on the other expenses. The average prices paid in specialty shops for the 1996-97 season

Photo by Trevor Graves; Rider: Satu Jarvela

"**F**ame and glory are nice, but I just want to go back and play with the mountain now. That's the real fun. Just ride for yourself and it will come. I never wanted to do contests or get sponsored when I started. It's just when you're motivated, there's no stopping you—that was surprising. So much speed, flow. . . it makes you kind of fearless when you start. Even when I fell on my head, I just kept riding."

—Nicole Angelrath, 26, Le Lauderon, Switzerland,

five-time World Halfpipe Champion

were $309 for a board, $132 for bindings, and $162 for boots, according to the 1997 Retail Audit by the SIA. Overproduction since then has resulted in a product glut and has forced prices down throughout the industry. Entry-level equipment is the least expensive (prices can be as low as $129 for a new, basic board); high-performance decks, like pro models from popular manufacturers made with top-quality materials, cost considerably more (closer to $500). In either case, you can take advantage of early- and late-season discounts rather than shopping between Thanksgiving and Christmas, when prices are at their highest. Spring closeouts, discontinued models, and secondhand gear also are significantly cheaper. Check your neighborhood snowboard and ski shops for a sale rack, as well as community "swap" events for quality used goods. Keep in mind that quality women's gear wasn't widely available until recently, so older equipment may not be appropriate for you. (See Chapter 5 for tips on selecting the right gear.)

Lift tickets also are significantly discounted early and late in the season, and tickets tend to cost less on weekdays than on weekends. For a long weekend or vacation, multi-day tickets can be cheaper than buying by the day, and the punch-card ticket system allows you to skip a day if the weather turns. Half-day tickets also are an option; they're widely available for a morning, afternoon, or even a few hours of night riding.

Finally, lodging and transportation packages offer all kinds of discounts, sometimes with lift tickets included. (Tour operators are the way to go to find a package

"I'm on chairlift #8 at Mount Snow in Vermont, a borrowed snowboard dangling from my left foot, the bright April sun's warmth helping me temporarily forget my sore, wet body. I look over to my companion on the lift and see smiling back at me a scrappy twelve-year-old boy. 'Rad sticker,' he declares, looking at my newly placed "Ride Like A Girl" sticker. He smiles approval. For a moment I forget my age, my gender, my responsibilities. I wonder how I appear to this kid. My blonde hair stuffed in under a hat, my face hidden under Oakleys, my body disguised by my baggy coat and pants. I could be any age, any gender. But I'm not. Here I am, a 29-year-old woman who, after only three days, is ready to trade in her world for the flight on the board. I am, as they say, stoked to be here."

—Amy Speace, singer,
song-writer from New York City

that suits your needs.) Chambers of Commerce and resort websites can also be great sources of information, particularly for those last-minute deals when you're chasing a snowstorm.

9.   **It's not just for punks anymore.** Once portrayed as the province of an underground few, snowboarding has grown from stepchild to supersport. As late as the early 1990s it was tough to find many other snowboarders on the mountain, not to mention girlfriends to ride with. Many resorts didn't like the "look" of the sport and banned it outright, while others required special certification tests if you wanted to "board" the lift. Even then, the ride often was restricted to a few, limited trails.

All of that has changed. Everyone is riding now—not just skaters and surfers, but your neighbors, their kids, and the IBM guy down the street. Even Dan Quayle (yikes) has tried it. Skiers, spurred by filmmaker Warren Miller's charge that "if snowboarding had been invented first, they wouldn't let skiers on the mountain," have gone from dissing "knuckledraggers" to converting in numbers big enough to panic the ski industry (which, in the sincerest form of flattery, responded by introducing "super-sidecut" skis modeled after alpine snowboards). At the resorts, banning and certification have all but disappeared, while halfpipes, snowboard parks, and other facilities designed specifically to attract snowboarders are multiplying. Early supporters like Stratton, in Vermont, and Mt. Baker, in Washington, have become Meccas of snowboarding activity, while the few remaining holdouts watch their bottom lines whither. (See the Resources section, page 137, for a list of snowboard-friendly resorts.) Even the business community is going gaga: Pepsi, Benetton, and Nike are investing in their own snowboard brands; Wall Street is buying into publicly traded manufacturing firms like Ride and Morrow; and major ad agencies like BBDO New York are pitching snowboard footage in their Super Bowl commercials. And, just 10 years after its first genuinely international competition,

Who says kids get to have all the fun? Women Only Snowboard Campers pause between runs for a Kodak moment. Riders: (back row) Evita Lagard, coach Julia Carlson, Karen Cha, Amy Speace, (front row) Mary McKhann, coach Tabbatha Henry, director Katie Bush. (Photo by Madelyn Bradley)

In the early '90s, Japanese women started snowboarding in such great numbers that shops, resorts, and manufacturers around the globe scrambled to attract their business. It is a little-known fact in the United States that early explosions in product offerings for women were due in large part to demand from Japan. Here Yoshiko Machida competes in the Super G at the U.S. Open at Stratton.

snowboarding was introduced as a medal sport in the 1998 Winter Olympic Games in Nagano, Japan.

Put it all together and snowboarding has indeed "arrived." Still less than a third the size of the ski industry, it nevertheless is the fastest-growing sport in the United States, with similar followings in Europe, Japan, Australia, and New Zealand. Women in particular are participating in record numbers in Japan as well as in the United States.

Okay, I lied—that's only nine reasons. The scenery in the mountains, the connection with your riding buddies, the excuse to go someplace you've never been—there are too many reasons left to pick just one more. Besides, part of the beauty of snowboarding is that everyone's list is different. Beginners and experts, freestylers and alpine riders, old-school and new-school—the styles are different but the stoke is the same, and it crosses all kinds of silly boundaries. So, welcome. It looks like Number 10 is up to you.

Chapter 2

YOUR FIRST TIME: TIPS FOR A SUCCESSFUL DEBUT

Photo by Patty Segovia; Riders: Michelle Yu, Donna Vano, Tara Dakides, CaraBeth Burnside

A little planning can make all the difference when it comes to your first day on a snowboard. Wearing the right clothes and protective gear will keep you toasty and comfortable, and locating a board/boot/binding setup that fits will have you riding like a champ in no time. Of course the pilot is as important as the plane, so it also helps to prepare yourself and to secure the help of a knowledgeable instructor. Ignore these seemingly simple truths and your first time can be downright painful. Heed them, on the other hand, and you'll be setting up for a great time.

WHAT AM I GONNA WEAR?

With respect to clothing, the goal is to keep yourself warm and dry when Mother Nature may have other plans. The first threat, of course, is from temperatures that can dip to well below freezing. Throw in the fact that all that snow has a tendency to melt on your clothes, and that you have a tendency to perspire, and snowboarding starts to look like a good way to become a human popsicle.

Luckily, the antidote is as simple as a little glorified polyester. Not to be confused with the cheesy stuff, high-tech synthetic clothing fabrics are good looking, comfortable, and warm enough

hat

jacket

fleece

long
underwear
top and
bottom

glove

outer pants

boots

heavy socks

Long underwear made from special polyesters looks and feels great, provides warmth even when wet, and wicks moisture away from your body.

Synthetic fleece and pile "insulators" provide all the warmth of wool or silk in lightweight fabrics that are soft, machine washable, and stay warm when wet.

Snowboard-specific outerwear is lightweight, cut for comfort, and made with hi-tech waterproof/breathable fabrics.

The warmest, driest clothing combination for a day of snowboarding is three layers of synthetic fibers.

to keep you cozy in the craziest conditions. The ones designed to go next to your skin wick moisture away from your body, provide warmth even if they're wet, and dry quickly. These go under synthetic, insulating layers like fleece pullovers and vests, which are also built to offer superior wicking, warmth, and drying. Top this off with synthetic outerwear that is waterproof, breathable, and windproof, and there is no warmer, dryer clothing combination.

Outer layer: special waterproof/breathable fabrics (see detail page 105)

Middle or insulating layer = fleece. Offers all the warmth of wool, silk or down, but it's lighter, snappy-dry, stays warm even when wet, and it **wicks**

First layer: 100% polyester-based fabric built for maximum **wicking** ability and warmth

Moisture Management = Wicking Plus Water Resistance/Water Proofing

Repeat: Choose synthetic fibers! Wool will do in a pinch, but synthetics are itchless, lighter, machine washable, and a snap to dry in comparison (kinda handy after a day on the hill, especially if you're likely to do a little laundry in the hotel sink). Cotton is an absolute no-no, even for die-hard natural-fiber fans. Those ubiquitous cotton turtlenecks will absorb water and freeze, leaving you with clammy crinkles against your neck and back. (Just ask my mom, who shivered through 25 years of Vermont winters before we could convince her to switch. When she actually made plans to give up and move to the islands, we outfitted her head-to-toe in synthetics and coaxed her into a one-day trial. We haven't seen her since; she's still out playing in the snow.)

Starting from the inside, a standard layering sequence is a long-sleeved, T-shirt-style top and not-quite-tight long underwear next to your skin, plus one sturdy pair of socks. Depending on the weather and your personal thermometer, each of these items is widely available in light-, mid-, and heavyweight options. Pop a fleece over the top and, on a normal day, you're already warm enough for the car ride to the mountain.

The colder it gets, the more layers you'll need to add for insulation. A couple of thin layers can be worth more than one bulky piece when it comes to keeping you cozy, plus you get more freedom of movement. The options are endless, but my favorites are a lightweight tank top (all warmth and zero bulk), an additional long-sleeved T-top that's slightly heavier than the first, and an extra pair of leggings made of dense, lightweight, windproof fleece. (All these items are useful in the off season for hiking, biking, sailing, and such, and they can be the key to survival through a cold winter under street clothes.) Vests are handy, too, especially if you happen to own one anyway, though shirts are easier to tie around your waist if things warm up on the hill. The only place to resist multiple layers is on your feet, where the temptation to load up on bulky socks will only make it difficult to control your board. For optimum warmth, response, and circulation, one sturdy pair is the way to go.

Finally, you'll need the right stuff on the outside. "Waterproof" and "breathable" are the prime features to look for in quality outerwear, so all that melting snow you're playing in can't get next to your hide. Alison Napolitano, former women's outerwear product manager for Burton Snowboards, explains: "Expect to see both 'waterproof' and 'water-resistant' labels. Waterproof means taped seams, special membranes inside the fabric, and/or high-quality brushed-on coatings that offer the highest levels of protection. Water-resistant pieces are much cheaper, because the raw materials are less expensive. The drawback is they won't stand up to the same conditions. You'll be fine on a normal day, but you will get wet if it rains."

Breathability is equally important. When you work up a sweat and your fancy underwear wicks the moisture off your skin, that moisture needs to be able to escape through your outerwear in order to evaporate. Otherwise you'll eventually feel clammy and uncomfortable (or worse if you're not well insulated). (Also look for handy outer jacket features like pit zips, back vents, and a stowaway hood, and pants with side zips—all good for dumping excess body heat.)

As for cut, choose a long jacket if you want extra rear-end coverage, or a shorter cut if you like the feel of extra mobility. Lots of pockets are also useful for keys, lunch money, lip stuff, and all the other necessities you might want to bring along. Pants with enough room for freedom of movement, plus a reinforced butt area for those moments on your derriere, are ideal. Stretch pants are out no matter how cute your tush, for the simple reason that there's not a lot of room for layers underneath. Besides, they limit your freedom of movement.

Top it all off with a hat, gloves, and goggles. (Don't be fooled by silly pictures of ski-bunny models without hats—unless it's spring or you ride in southern California, you'll want everything down to your earlobes covered.) You lose a dispro-

(Photo by Patty Segovia)

Left: Pro rider Barrett Christy makes her goggle sponsor proud. **Below:** Fleece hats provide itch-free warmth. **Right:** For cozy fingers all day long, choose windproof, waterproof gloves or mittens.

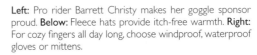

portionate amount of body heat through your head, so, "If your toes are cold, put a hat on," as the saying goes. Ditto for your fingers, which will benefit from the best waterproof protection you can afford. (For extra warmth, go for mittens over gloves, or add a layer of thin, synthetic glove liners.) And don't forget your neck: Lots of snowboarders won't leave home without a neck warmer. Finally, look for the new women's goggles—the frames are designed to be small enough to fit your face.

> "The only place to resist multiple layers is on your feet, where the temptation to load up on bulky socks will only make it difficult to control your board."

So where do you find all these goodies and what's it going to do to your wallet? If you are at all active in the outdoors, the first place to check is your closet. Just about everything but the goggles can be useful for all kinds of things besides snowboarding (and vice versa). The tights or pants you originally bought for running, hiking, or biking are likely crossover candidates; so are your tops (as long as neither contains any cotton). How's your jacket collection? Rubber is strictly for raincoats and windshirts are strictly for running, but something in between might be just the waterproof/breathable combo you need for a shell. Then all you'll need is plenty of insulation underneath.

If your existing wardrobe doesn't yield much, almost any outdoor outfitter can supply most of the essentials. Snowboard specialty shops are your best bet for one-stop shopping and they're probably the most likely place to find experienced help. Most ski shops and outdoor stores also stock quality gear, but they tend to cater to more "classic" tastes. Large chain stores can be cheaper, but don't count on the sales staff to help you weed through the lesser-quality stuff. Ditto for some of the big mail-order catalogs: They're a great place for variety, economy, and tough-to-find sizes, but you need to know what to look for.

You'll need some cash to pay for all the clothing, probably to the tune of a few hundred bucks if you're really starting from scratch. But hey—clear blue sky or raging snowstorm, you'll never have to be cold again. Shop early or late in the season for discounts, and watch for sales or promotions at your local shops. Sometimes all it takes is an inquiry—maybe there's a "local's" discount or a package deal on sets. Finally, consider a trip to the second-hand store. I dunno about hand-me-down underwear, but good outerwear lasts a long time.

CHOOSING YOUR RIDE

Shops and manufacturers are getting better than ever about providing gear that works well for women. Still, even the best rental shops can run short of the right models and sizes in a Saturday morning rush, and well-meaning friends can have the best of intentions without the right spare gear. A few key features can mean the difference between a safe, comfortable virgin experience and a seriously bruised tailbone, so it's important to know what to look for.

Top: Snowboard boots may look a lot like street stuff on the outside, but they are built with all kinds of special features. **Middle:** Step-in systems use an automated mechanism built into the sole of your boot (as opposed to a binding with straps) to hold your foot to the board. For better heel hold, look for a system with an ankle strap on the boot. **Bottom:** Hard boots are literally less forgiving than soft boots, which makes them less suitable for beginners.

Boots

Snowboard boots may look a lot like street stuff on the outside, but don't be fooled—they're designed with all kinds of special features to help you ride well. Be sure you get snowboard-specific boots that are "soft-" as opposed to "hard-" shelled. Soft boots are literally more forgiving, which is what makes them better for beginners. You may also have a choice between a *step-in* or *strap* boot-and-binding system. Step-in systems are a bit like clipless bike shoes and pedals: Your feet are held to the board by a retention mechanism built into the sole of the boot (as opposed to strap-type bindings, which feature external straps that go over the top of your foot). While this makes them more convenient, it can also compromise their ability to hold your foot flat against the board. For now, most of the world's pros still choose straps. (The section on bindings provides more information on binding styles and choices.)

It's also critical to get a boot made especially for women. You need a snug fit to control your board and (as with underwear) guy's stuff is just a lot different. Women's feet tend to be smaller and narrower through the ankle as well as the forefoot, and so are good women's boots. We also tend to have larger lower calf muscles, so women's boots have cool features like flared liners for comfortable support. Ask for them specifically and be sure to try them on to check out the fit.

Once you've got 'em on, be sure your boots pass the "tiptoe test": Start by lacing them good and tight, particularly over the ankle, then stand up on your tiptoes and try to lift your heels inside the boot. If they stay snug in the heel pocket, you're good to go. If not, it's going to be tough to control your board. See if you can get them tighter by hauling hard on the laces and/or on any "power straps" at the ankles. If you're still swimming in them, it's time to look for a different boot. Try a size smaller or another brand—as with running shoes or sneakers, you may have to go up or down a bit from your usual shoe size, and different brands sometimes fit better on certain feet. One last note: It may seem tempting to throw on an extra pair of bulky socks, either for warmth or to fill up big boots. Don't. You'll be much more comfortable, have better control, and probably even be warmer with one pair of sturdy socks and boots that fit "like a glove."

Freestyle

Freeride

Alpine

Left: Freestyle boards tend to be relatively short and wide, and rounded up at both ends for easy riding forward or switch (backward). **Center:** Freeriding boards are longer and narrower, with bigger noses for flotation in powder. **Right:** Alpine or carving boards are longer and narrower still, with low profile noses and a squared-off tail.

Board and bindings

"Women's" boards are available if you prefer, and some women-specific models are really terrific. Others are nothing special except for the label, and there are plenty of "unisex" boards out there that were designed and tested with women in mind. I say skip the marketing hype—let's take a look at the toys.

Boards come in a variety of lengths and shapes. Dimensions like the overall length are usually measured in centimeters, and range from about 140 cm (relatively short for an adult) to over 165 cm (for big experts only). Shapes also vary, from relatively short and wide boards (made for *freestyle* riding in the halfpipe and terrain park), to super-long and skinny boards (for alpine riding, called *carving*). In between are *freeriding* boards, which tend to feature more moderate lengths and widths for better all-mountain performance.

What you want to start with is a freeriding board that's about shoulder high, with a midsection (or *waist width*) that's the same size as your feet. The height check is simple: Stand the board on end in front of you and pull it up under your chin. (The board may come with bindings already mounted, in which case you'll want to point those away from your body while the flat base goes against your chest.) Now—which part of your body is approximately level with the top of the board? If it's your nose, the board is probably long enough to be difficult to maneuver, like learning to drive in a truck. But you don't want something you couldn't hide behind in a demi-bra. Modesty aside, you need a board that's above-boob high for stability.

Then it's time to look at how the bindings are mounted on the board. The rental shop (or the friend you're borrowing from) will need to know if you're *regular* (left foot forward) or *goofy* (right foot forward) so the bindings can be mounted properly. Consider which foot is forward when you bat, kick a ball, or run-and-slide on ice. Most people heavily favor one side; others really can't tell until they've

Board height between chest and chin

Board width= length of your foot

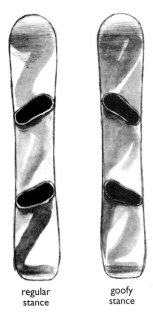

regular
stance

goofy
stance

A "regular" stance means left foot forward. Riding "goofy" means right foot forward.

had a chance to try both stances. Don't worry if you're not sure; just take your best guess and go with it. Snowboard bindings are designed to be switched around easily, so if you wind up more comfortable going backwards you can always come back for a fix.

Once the board is set up, it's time for a test drive. Slap that puppy down on the rental shop floor (or the living room carpet, whichever is handy) and jump right on it. Don't let the bindings intimidate you; you can step around them at first if necessary, or walk up and down the thing just to get a feel for it. Take your time and get oriented. Think of it like taking the driver's seat in someone else's car—there's nothing wrong with taking a minute to find the lights and blinkers, adjust the mirrors, and so on.

When you're ready, place one foot in each binding and buckle in. You'll need your boots on (chances are you're wearing them at this point, anyway). This step may be easier if there's a bench or counter handy, or at least a friendly person around to lean on. Don't be shy—you might feel a little awkward or conspicuous, but take the time and space. For jeans you get a dressing room; for cars you get a road; for snowboards you might have to improvise.

Once you're buckled in, take a few minutes to get a feel for things—it's a nice preview of what it will feel like standing on the hill, minus the difficulty of a slippery slope. (Not to mention it's a great head start on the buddy you're meeting for a lesson.)

Now for some questions. First, how does that stance feel? Is the correct foot forward? Do you have any painful pressure points, maybe something digging into your calf? (Standing sideways may be awkward but you shouldn't feel any pain.) Remember, bindings in particular are designed to be customized to the rider, so it's reasonable to expect that yours may need some fine-tuning. (The section on cutomizing your ride, page 109–116, tells you just how to do it.)

Now also is the time to double-check the midsection of your board: The board should be about as wide as your feet are long, and the bindings need to be positioned so that your toes and heels sit directly over the edges. It's easy to see if your setup doesn't fit: Just look at the toe and heel of each of your boots to see if they're lined up directly over the edges of the board. If so, you're good to go. If not, there are two likely problems:

- **Overhang.** If either the toe or heel of your boot extends out past the edge of the board it will drag in the snow like an anchor.

- **Underhang.** Just the opposite: A gap of up to an inch or so between the end of your boot and the edge of the board will make balancing over the edge about as easy as riding a picnic table.

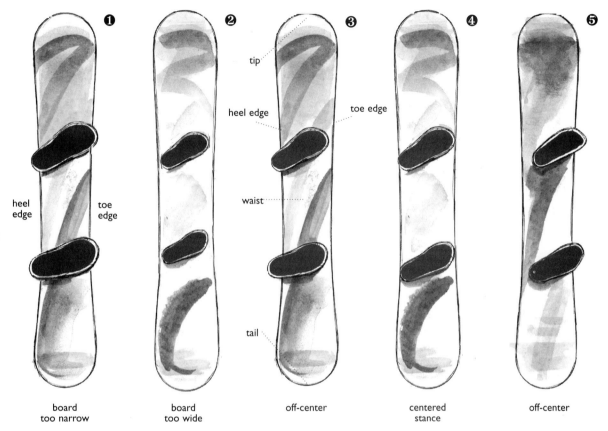

tip

heel edge   toe edge

heel
edge   toe
edge

waist

tail

❶   **❷**   **❸**   **❹**   **❺**

board
too narrow   board
too wide   off-center   centered
stance   off-center

Board width (1 and 2) and **binding position** (3, 4, and 5) are other factors to consider when checking out a board. A centered stance (4) means your toes and heels are lined up over the edges. This provides optimum balance and leverage, whereas off-center stances make it harder to turn and balance (3 and 5).

If your boots are not lined up precisely over the edges, make the adjustments now—it won't take long. As many women discover on their very first day, a couple of seemingly tiny adjustments can make a huge difference in your riding. Consider Beth Muzzy, a 24-year-old midwife and nursing student from Burlington, Vermont. At first, her heels were hanging off the board and her toes didn't quite reach the opposite edge, so we stopped in the middle of a run and moved her bindings over. Then we noticed that the highback on her binding was digging into her calf, so we stopped to fix that as well. It only took a minute to make each adjustment, but the difference in her riding was huge. "At first I thought it was overkill," says Beth, but "I could really feel the difference with every little adjustment." Sure enough, her balance improved immediately, as did both her heel- and toeside turns.

Finally, be sure that your bindings hold your feet flat against the board. This part is a little like the tiptoe test for boots: Strap or click into your bindings and try to pick your heels up off the board, and try lifting your toes and the balls of your feet. If your feet are not held firmly against the board in both places, it's going to be tough to turn. Assuming that your boots are laced nice and snug already, try cranking down a few notches on any binding straps. Heel lift in a conventional strap binding probably means the last customer was bigger than you are, so see if someone can adjust the straps better. Step-in binding systems by definition do not have any straps, so now is the time to be doubly sure that the boot itself can hold your foot down. Finally, some boots and bindings offer a third strap that goes around your shin. These are fine (though not necessary); they don't need to be as tight as the straps that hold your feet to the board.

RIDER PROFILE

ALI ZACAROLI

East Coast surf diva and PR coordinator at SnowSports Industries America, the industry trade association in McLean, Virginia.

Age: 29
Height: 5'1"
Weight: 105
Foot Size: 6
Years Riding: 6

BOOTS AND BINDINGS ◄---

Ali swears by the new Switch Millennium step-in binding and boot. Her boots are a size 6, the same as her street-shoe size, which says a lot about Switch fit. "The boot is built around a Ferragamo last. It's the most comfortable boot I've ever ridden, conventional setups included."

As for step-in versus strap bindings, Ali is one of the few experienced testers of both systems to prefer a step-in above everything else: "It's a matter of finding the system that you're going to like and feel comfortable with. Step-in technology has come so far—there are a lot of people who tried step-ins two years ago and got turned off, but they're completely different today. Maybe they're not right for pros who can feel every little thing in their equipment, but for the average rider there's really not much of a difference."

BOARD ◄---

Ali rides a Bev Sanders 148 from Avalanche. "I'm really lucky in that I get to try everything out there," she says. "I like the Sanders 148 because I have really small feet. It's one of the few boards narrow enough to initiate turns easily, and yet still long enough not to chatter at high speeds. It stays steady and stable, which is hard to find in a woman's board. It's a real problem—most of them are so short and soft they chatter around as you pick up speed."

"Don't let your boyfriend pick out what you're going to do. I see it all the time. I know it seems like you need a Ph.D. at first, but it's important to do your own research. Guys just don't know what it's like to have your needs, and if you have bad equipment it's going to ruin your experience. Go to all the shops you can and ask lots of questions. Find someone knowledgeable who will spend lots of time with you—not some kid who just started working there, but someone who has been riding since the beginning. Find a girl to talk to. Ask a lot of questions in each place because you'll get a variety of answers. Then just draw your best conclusions. Oh yeah, and go to on-snow demos! Then you don't have to take anyone's word for it— you can try everything for yourself. They don't always have women's boots, so make some noise about that, and then next year you can really try everything for yourself."

—Stacie Genchi, founder and co-owner of On Edge Girl's Board Shop in Huntington Beach, California

Top: Tabbatha Henry, customer service rep for Burton Snowboards, test drives a helmet on the steeps of Tuckerman's Ravine. (Photo by Mike Artz) **Right:** Alaskan speed queen Rosey Fletcher shows off the diamond embedded in her front tooth (top row, 2nd from center). "It's just something she wanted to do," says Dad, who must be glad she didn't opt for a tattoo. (Photo by Barrie Fisher/Sports File Photography)

PROPHYLACTICS (I COULDN'T RESIST)

As for protective gear, consider wrist guards, knee pads, and butt protection. Studies show that wrist injuries are by far the most common for beginners, and that wrist guards can reduce the risk of injury by 50 percent. Snowboard-specific gloves are available with built-in wrist protection. The same ones you use for in-line skating will also work if you can find gloves or mittens to fit over them.

Equipment expert Ali Napolitano points out that padding also is important for beginners: "One option is snowboard pants with removable padding in the knees and butt area. A few companies also make first-layer pieces with built-in padding. There's a brand called Numb with pads in the knees, hips, butt, and thigh. They feel great and look terrific." There is also a brand called Crash Pads (see resource guide).

If you're not ready to invest in specific equipment for your first time out, stand-alone knee pads (like those used for in-line skating or skateboarding) also are fine, and most can go over or under your pants. As for your derriere, a pair of bike shorts can be a good start. After that, feel free to get creative—I've heard of a number of imaginative solutions involving everything from shoulder pads to hockey shorts.

Finally, helmets are gaining popularity for snowboarding, just as they have for cycling. No need to worry about feeling conspicuous if you've got the urge to protect your noggin—in fact, it's a great idea for the first few times out. New helmets can get expensive, though, so try a rental. More and more shops are starting to carry helmets in adult sizes, though if nothing else they might have a kid's version that will work.

PREPPING THE PILOT

The better the shape you're in, the easier it's going to be to ride. Not that any specific minimum conditioning is required—the sport doesn't have to be physically demanding—but a few trips to the gym before you head for the mountain can make a big difference in your confidence and comfort.

I'm no personal trainer but I did do a lot of training as a pro rider, and what follows is my present warm-up routine for the season (keep in mind I'm just an old fart now). It's an easy, 60- to 90-minute workout, two or three times a week, which I try to do for at least six weeks before snow flies.

1.   **Warm-up and aerobic workout.** Almost any aerobic activity will do, whether it's jazz class, Tae Kwon Do, or your basic step aerobics. (I also like to jump on the Stairmaster for 25 to 30 minutes. All of its programs have a built-in 5-minute warm up; then bump up to whatever level of challenge you decide you're up to that day.) Whatever aerobic activity you choose, it's not necessary to send your heart rate through the roof. Do make sure you break a sweat, and tune in to the Weather Channel (there's nothing like a forecast of snow for motivation).

2.   **Strength training.** I do a bare-bones routine of squats, lunges, sit-ups, bench presses, and lat pull-downs. Other strength routines are fine but these exercises are the staples.

I strongly recommend using freeweights, though they are harder to use correctly than most Universal or Nautilus machines. The benefit is that you learn to stabilize the load yourself, as opposed to depending on a machine to do it for you. This is exactly what you'll need to do when snowboarding, so the *practice* of using freeweights is just as important as the *amount of weight* you lift. Be sure to get step-by-step guidance from someone at the gym—and go light on the weights until you can handle the movements smoothly.

3. **Explosive training.** If you happen to be used to a challenging workout, try some "box jumps." I used to train with a team in Colorado where the strongest athletes on the hill were almost invariably the ones who could do the most box jumps in the gym. Set up a box about two-thirds the height of your shin (step-aerobics boxes work fine) and stand on it facing one of the narrow ends. Keeping your feet together, jump down to the floor on one side, back up to the center of the box, down to the other side, and back up again. Pause on top of the box until you get a rhythm going, and then start counting. Pack in as many jumps as you can in 30 or 60 seconds (depending on how long you can last) and then work your way up to 90 seconds. This is an incredibly intense anaerobic workout that I only recommend for people in excellent health.

4. **Cool down and stretch.** If your Stairmaster program, aerobics, or Tae Kwon Do class doesn't end with a cool-down session, try a slow jog or bike ride for 10 minutes, followed by a very important stretch routine. As Dr. Robert K. Cooper recommends in *Health and Fitness Excellence*, try finishing up with a couple of tighten-relax-stretch postures. As he says, "Dynamic flexibility exercises are smooth, easy movements that increase ranges of motion for the joints of the body. Tighten-relax-stretch exercises tense a muscle or group of muscles for 10 to 30 seconds, followed by 2 to 3 seconds of relaxation, and then a gentle stretching action for 10 to 30 seconds. This stretching method gives a surprisingly fast and effective increase in flexibility and works well for people of all ages." See a trainer at your local gym for professional instruction.

LOCATION, LOCATION, LOCATION

Choosing the right place for your first snowboarding adventure is largely a matter of taste. It doesn't have to be a major resort—any hill with a nicely groomed beginner slope and a snowboard-friendly attitude will do. The beginner slope should be classified as "easiest" according to international trail conventions, and it also should have a dedicated chairlift. (Surface lifts like T-bars and pomas, originally designed to carry skiers, are generally not a good idea for beginning snow-

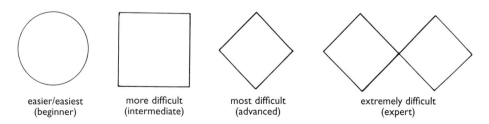

easier/easiest   more difficult   most difficult   extremely difficult
(beginner)   (intermediate)   (advanced)   (expert)

North American resorts use green circles, blue squares, and black diamonds to designate the degree of difficulty for most trails.

boarders—they tend to hit your body at some awkward, painful angle, and sliding up the hill in a snowboard stance is difficult unless the hill is perfectly sloped. Chairlifts are much more comfortable, and the ones that service beginner trails exclusively tend to run nice and slow. Everyone has plenty of time to get on and off, and there's often an extra attendant or two to help out. See pages 41–44 for more on riding the lifts.)

Snowboard-friendliness is also a key feature to look for. Be sure your destination isn't one of the rare holdouts that continue to ban snowboarding, such as Taos Ski Valley (New Mexico), Mad River Glen (Vermont), or Alta (Utah). Some resorts may not ban snowboarding outright, but those who merely tolerate it can be limited in terms of quality rentals, experienced instructors, and allowing snowboarders full access to the mountain. Be sure to check for these basics and ask about special facilities (like a halfpipe or terrain park) if you want some expert inspiration. Finally, some resorts have emerged as snowboarding "hot spots." If you really want to see some action, check around for snowboarding events at a deluxe resort near you. (Snowboard-friendly resorts are listed on pages 137–138.)

Also, keep in mind that some resorts offer special lift tickets for beginners. If you're sure you'll stick to the "bunny slope," tickets exclusively for the beginner lift may be significantly cheaper than those for full-mountain access. Package deals, like Stowe's "Hook-a-Rookie" program—which includes lift access, instruction, and equipment rental for as little as $75 for three days—are also available. Contact a variety of resorts to find the best deals around, and remember: Things get expensive on holidays. You're likely to get a better deal on weekdays or off-peak weekends, particularly early or late in the season.

Finally, it might be worthwhile to check into "demo days," when manufacturers' reps come to a resort, set up all the latest goodies right at the bottom of the slopes, and let you try whatever you want. Best of all, it's free! Check with a local snowboard shop for coming attractions in the area, or look in catalogs and snowboard magazines for a calendar of events near you.

PLAN ON A HALF DAY

It's longer than your average gym session but shorter than a full day on the slopes. Why shoot the middle? On the one hand, your first time out is the time to take it slow and give yourself ample opportunity to learn. Anything less and you'll likely miss out on the fun of linking your very first turns. Stay much longer, on the other hand, and exhaustion may set in. It's tough to leave when you're making progress (and you will, quickly), but it's smart. Your muscles will thank you in the morning, when you'll be fresh enough to contemplate going again. You wouldn't start running with a marathon, so stick with that half day at first.

It's also a great idea to commit to three tries ahead of time. Standing sideways with both feet attached takes some getting used to, and you'll probably spend a good part of your first day on the ground. It's nice to anticipate your second experience, which will be twice the fun, right away. By the third time out you'll feel positively proficient (and maybe even suspend the "no camera" rule). Finally, lift tickets and rentals are usually discounted when you buy two or three days at a time.

Women Only Snowboard Campers pose for a victory shot after conquering the bunny slope. Left to right: Dr. Laurie Spina (NJ), Claire Moore Dickerson (NY), camper-turned-coach Maureen O'Keefe (MA), coach Julia Carlson (VT), Kim Lukes (MI), coach Bilynda Wiggins (MA), Melissa DeCarlo (TX), and Peggy Sarkela (CT).

BRING A BUDDY

There's nothing like the trial of your first snowboard lesson for a bonding experience, and having familiar company to laugh with can make the whole day more fun. Best friends are good candidates, since you won't mind humiliating yourselves in each other's company, and they also can be great road-trip companions.

Kids are likely copilots, too. Since the myth that snowboarding is dangerous has disappeared, more and more families are learning the sport together. If mom is game, you know the kids will go, and it's only a matter of time until dad signs on. (I have yet to see three generations at once, but I'm looking.) Equipment should be widely available to fit kids down to age four or five, though some as young as two years old are snowboarding. Call the rental shop ahead of time to be sure they stock gear for the kids, as well as children's helmets if you're interested. Some resorts have minimum-age requirements for lessons; if you're planning on instruction for the kids, be sure to check this as well.

GET SOME HELP

The right instructor can do wonders for your skills in just a couple of hours. Private lessons are ideal—you get the instructor all to yourself—but group lessons tend to be much cheaper. Plus there's nothing like a bunch of other floundering folks to lift your spirits in a moment of frustration. Ask at a few resorts to get options.

"**D**efinitely take a lesson. It takes a lot of time off the learning process. Also, ride with people who are better than you. That's what I did, and it's a great way to push yourself."

—Barrett Christy, one of the top pro riders in North America

• •

"I've heard so many stories about people who had a bad experience learning to snowboard. I had such an awesome experience—I didn't get hurt, I had a great time, and I made progress quickly. I totally attribute that to having a great instructor, so I'm a big advocate of getting a lesson!"

—Ali Napolitano

• •

Keep in mind that unless you specify otherwise, resort schools tend to classify students according to ability level. Classes targeted at women and/or exclusively adults may be available, and they tend to be smaller. Don't forget to look for a package deal that includes equipment rental, and ask about other beginner specials.

Consider a *snowboard camp* as an alternative to the traditional lessons you book through resorts. Like summer camps for kids, a camp can offer more of a group experience both on and off the mountain. Two popular options for women are Wild Women Snowboard Camps out of Jackson Hole, Wyoming, and Women Only Snowboard Camps in Sugarbush, Vermont. Both have weekend and multi-day packages suited to a variety of ability levels, with the primary attraction being the opportunity to learn in the company of other women. As WOSC camper Maureen O'Keefe, 27, explains, the environment can have its advantages: "It definitely wasn't about posing or trying to meet guys. I knew I wanted to learn to ride, I had the money, and a women's camp seemed like an atmosphere that was fun and easy to be around. I also liked the idea of learning from a woman and not having any of the macho distractions of a mixed group." Judging by the grin on her face as she spun 360s down the mountain (this great drill is described on pages 64–65), Maureen got what she came for.

Chapter 3

LET'S GO RIDE: THE BASICS

Photo by Patty Segovia; Rider: Tara Dakides

First things first: Before you worry about sideslipping, turning, or stopping, you need to know how to buckle into your bindings, skate with your back foot, and ride the lift.

Start by finding a nice flat stretch of snow at the bottom of a hill and buckling or clicking in only your front foot. If you are riding strap bindings, tighten the ankle strap firmly first—it'll pull your foot back into the binding—and then fasten your toe strap. If you are riding step-ins, tighten any power straps at the ankle of the boot. The point is to be sure your heel and toes are snug against the board. *Also, be sure to fasten the safety leash if there's one attached to your binding.*

When buckling into strap bindings, always fasten your ankle strap first.

SKATING

Once your front foot is in, you'll need to get the hang of pushing yourself around using your back foot. Be sure you're in an uncrowded, flat section of snow, pick a spot in front of you, and steer the board with your front foot as you push off with your back one. Take small steps at first, as this is a whole new kind of motion for most people. (If you have skateboarding experience this movement probably will come quite easily.) It helps to look ahead, not down at your feet, and to put your arms out a bit for balance. It also helps to keep your weight on your front foot, to keep your front knee bent, and to keep your board flat on the snow.

Pro rider Betsy Shaw demonstrates **skating**. "This will feel a bit awkward at first but just go with it," says Betsy, "and soon it will actually begin to feel normal."

The pivot

The next thing to try is turning around using your free foot as a pivot while you lift the board and pull it around with the foot that's buckled in. It sounds complicated, but it's really pretty easy: Just turn your free (back) foot a little (1), plant all your weight on it, and then lift the board around a little bit at a time using your front leg (2). (This is easier to do if you keep the board tilted up on its toeside edge, as opposed to flat on the snow.) Stop when you're facing in the opposite direction (3), and then try pivoting the other way around. (And make sure there's plenty of space between you and your riding buddies, unless you think it might be fun to get tangled up together on the ground.)

Gliding

Now it's time to speed up a little. With most of your weight on your front foot, keep the board flat on the snow and use your back foot to push hard, so you gain some momentum. Then place your back foot on the board, and transfer some weight to it for stability as you glide along. The ideal spot for your back foot is just behind your front binding, with the toe of your boot hanging over the edge so you can use it to stop or turn if necessary. Look for the non-skid *deck mat* or *stomp pad* between your bindings—it's there to keep your back foot from slipping as it rests on the board.

Once you slow to a stop, push off and ride it out again *with your back foot on the board*. Remember to keep the board flat by keeping your weight evenly distributed between your heel and toes, and try bending your knees. (Beginners tend to stiffen up and lock their legs, when in fact the opposite is necessary for good balance.) It helps to look ahead and to place your hands as if they're on a table in front of you. Take your time and keep practicing until you're comfortable with the motion, as gliding is the same technique you'll use for getting off the lift.

WALKING UPHILL

You may need to walk uphill a bit in order to get to the lift. In this case it doesn't work to point the nose of the board straight ahead—the board will just slip backwards down the hill. Instead, turn it sideways: Pivot 90 degrees so your *body* faces up the hill while the *board* points across it. Step forward with your free foot and tilt the board up on its toeside edge so it can't slip away from you. Then step up the hill, leading with your free foot and following with the board.

ROCKING THE CHAIRLIFT

Once you've got the hang of moving around with the board, you're ready for the chairlift. No, really! (Just be sure you've got the right one, with at least one trail marked "easiest" to bring you back down.)

look ahead not down

hands low and in front

back foot on deck mat

knees bent for balance

weight on forward foot

Pro rider Betsy Shaw demonstrates **gliding**. "Don't be afraid to commit your weight to that front foot," says Betsy. "Trust your balance and keep your foot relaxed."

Walking uphill: "Make sure to keep the board on edge to keep from sliding out," says Betsy.

"**D**on't give up! Don't be intimidated by what other people think,
or be afraid to look stupid. You
can't let that slow you down. The
first time I went it was all guys,
me, and my friend Beth
(Trombley). She's been my best
friend ever since."

—Tricia Byrnes, professional snowboarder
Greenwich, Connecticut

You're still buckled in with your front foot only, so skate slowly into the lift line, and make note of how many people ride the lift at once. If it's a *double* (only two people in the chair), you and your buddy will have plenty of room getting off; if it's a *triple* or *quad*, consider finding a place in line that puts you in one of the outside seats on the chair. You'll probably be less distracted with only one person beside you getting off.

When you reach the front of the line, watch as the chair in front of you is loaded. As soon as it has safely passed you, skate up behind it and then look back over your shoulder for the coming chair. As it comes up behind you, relax, don't hesitate, and sit down. If you want something to hold on to and you're on one end of the chair, grab the side support. If you're in the middle, you can grab the backrest until you're actually seated, but then you might feel a little twisted up so you'll want to let go. Don't be alarmed if someone falls, sits partially on your lap, or gets bumped a little and drops a pair of mittens. Chairlift attendants can stop the lift in a heartbeat with the press of a shiny red button if necessary; otherwise they'll just help you load safely and send those mittens up with the folks a chair or two behind you. There. Once you're in and comfortable don't forget to put the safety bar down.

Soon you're checking out the breathtaking view of all the other mountains behind you and watching all the other snowboarders riding below for pointers. If you haven't noticed the footrest on the safety bar, your board may start to feel a little heavy hanging there on one foot. Take a load off by placing the board on top of the little bar and you're set—unless there's no footrest, in which case it's surprisingly comfortable just to rest the tail of your board on the toe of your free foot.

Getting off

Uh, oh. Here comes the top. But that's okay because once the safety bar is up, all you really need to remember are the three Ps:

- **Point** your board straight ahead.
- **Place** it flat on the snow.
- **Place** your back foot on the board just behind the front one.

It's really that simple. What follows is a detailed blow-by-blow, just so you know how things will go down, but don't let it overwhelm you. You already know what to do!

The keys to a smooth exit: **1. Point** your board so the nose is facing straight ahead; **2. Place** your board flat against the snow at the top of the exit ramp; and **3. Place** your back foot on the board, then just stand up and coast out of the way.

So, you're nearing the top of the lift and someone pushes up the safety bar. The ground is a ways off yet so you grab a handy piece of chair for safety. That's cool; you can use it to steady yourself until there's land under your feet. (Hold on with just one hand—you may need the other to help you keep your balance.)

Soon you're there, staring at the ground, and you know it's time to get off. In a momentary fit of panic, everything you know about what you're supposed to do vanishes from your mind, replaced entirely by the urgent need to pee. Doh! There it is. Ah yes, "P." As in the three Ps, which you recall with relief. Once again the ground beneath you comes into focus, along with your board, which is hovering just above it. So you *point* your board straight ahead, and *place* it flat on the snow. You're still sitting on the chair, which is moving, but slowly. The board is sliding along on the ground underneath you, and as you look at it, a great big bullseye forms between the bindings. Whoa, cool. So you *place* your back foot on it, right smack in the middle, with maybe just a toe or two hanging over the edge.

Now it's time to stand up. Ack! Pressure! You're still way too wobbly for this! Not. Because you just practiced this part a dozen times at the bottom of the hill so you know exactly what to do: Transfer your weight to your feet, pick your

"**G**etting off the chair is one of the hardest tasks to master. Relaxing is key. Don't panic! And don't be discouraged if it takes a while to master—I still fall occasionally and have been in pro snowboarder hog piles at the top of lifts many times. Just laugh it off—the only thing it hurts is your ego."

—Betsy Shaw

T-BAR STRATEGIES
• • • • • • • • • • • • • • • •

Surface lifts like T-bars, which *tow* you up the mountain while you're standing on your board, are more difficult to ride than a chairlift. It's challenging to ride with one foot out, particularly when something is pulling you uphill, and the same bar that hits a skier in her well-padded booty can bruise the hipbone of someone turned sideways on a snowboard. If you have a choice, ride a chairlift. If you don't, try putting the T-bar between your legs (sideways) as you get on, so it pulls your front thigh from behind as opposed to bumping your hip bone. Then firm up all the muscles in your legs and abdomen, as if someone is about to push you and you don't want to budge. The T-bar gives a similar tug as it starts to pull you uphill, so staying firm will help keep you right-side up.

head up, bend those bolt-straight knees, and place your hands on the imaginary tabletop in front of you. Standing now, just as you did in the gliding exercise earlier, you coast effortlessly to safety down the gentle slope of the off ramp, which conveniently flattens out right away, stopping you automatically. Easy as pie.

Now, quick, turn around and laugh hysterically at the look on her face as the fellow beginner behind you goes through the same experience. And then move it, darlin', because chances are that in a few seconds she's gonna be right on your tail! Not to worry, just turn away from the exit ramp by taking your back foot off the board, pivoting on your free foot (just as you did at the bottom), and skating to the nearest flat spot. Phew. High five, sister—you made it.

The view from the top

Once you're safely out of the way of traffic exiting the chairlift, it's time for a good look around. Above you is the top station of the lift, with a huge wheel where all the chairs turn around and head back down the mountain. Below is the beginner slope, a trail with probably about as much pitch as the average highway ramp. It's wide open, with dips and rolls as it drops gently away. This one happens to have trees down both sides, like a country interstate, and a fresh layer of pristine snow for pavement. You

Riding the lift at the first annual Fresh Session, an all-girl snowboard pow-wow at Sugarbush, Vermont. Mother Nature blessed the event with 6 inches of fresh snow, and 150 women riders from all over the U.S. got first tracks together riding side by side. (Photo by Greg Greenwood, courtesy Fresh and Tasty.)

can almost see a broken yellow line down the middle, sprinkled on both sides with other people out making their first turns. Some navigate hesitantly; others zip back and forth, maybe a little too fast for comfort, already addicted to the adrenaline rush. Get ready to be a road hog—we're going straight down the middle.

BUCKLING IN

Find a flat spot near the middle of the trailhead and skate your way there. It's a whole lot easier to buckle in if you're sitting down, but you have to be in the right position first. This part is pretty intuitive once you get there, but just in case, it goes like this: Standing with your belly button facing directly down the mountain, place your board so it's facing sideways (*across the hill*) and resting on its heelside edge (the edge under your heels).

Once you've got your board sideways, step back with your free foot so it's on the uphill side of your board. That way the board won't catch you behind the knee as you lower yourself to the ground. Okay? Now have a seat.

Now you need to get your back foot into the binding. Start by tilting the board uphill so the top of it is facing you (this makes it a lot easier to get your foot all the way into the binding). Place your foot in the empty binding and, if you're in a conventional strap binding, buckle up nice and tight. Repeat: *tight*. Most beginners seem to tighten up only about half as much as they should, not realizing yet that a lot of serious wobbles will disappear instantly with tighter bindings. If you're in a step-in setup,

Betsy Shaw fastens her back binding nice and tight, so neither her heels nor toes will lift up off the board. "Don't let more experienced friends rush you," says Betsy. "Take the time to do it right."

"I thought riding with my boots and bindings loose would give me flexibility, like wearing loose clothes. Tight is so much better! I can actually feel the board now, which gives me so much more control. I'm not struggling anymore, and I can really feel every turn."

—Madelyn Bradley, 31, WOSC camper and freelance photographer from Philadelphia

look for an ankle strap attached to the boot that can be tightened down before you click in. Don't forget to tighten down your front foot as well. You can always loosen your bindings for the ride back up the lift, but for riding purposes you don't want to be able to lift the toes or heels of either foot off the board.

Reaching across and grabbing the far edge of your board makes it easier to stand up. "Edge control is important here," says Betsy. "Dig in those heels."

STANDING UP

Getting up can be awkward at first. The key is not to let the board slide away from you while you transfer your weight to your feet. This is accomplished in three ways:

- **Scooch into a tucked position** so the board is up close to your body. (This will make it easier to transfer your weight from your hips to your feet in one small motion.)

- **Dig the edge of the board into the snow** by flexing your feet and pressing down with your heels. (This is what keeps your board from moving.)

- **Reach across and grab the far edge** of the board with your back hand. (This helps keep the board tilted up, plus you can use it to pull yourself up.)

From there it's pretty straightforward. Lift your hips up so you're squatting over the board, using your front hand on the ground for stability. (This part feels a little like crab-walking, except you can't let your feet move.) Then straighten up just to the point where your knees are still bent, as if you just absorbed the impact of jumping off a stair.

Common stance problems: 1. Too tall (knees locked);
2. Too pooped (butt poking out the back); 3. Too stooped
(shoulders hunched over); 4. Ahh . . . just right (neutral or
"ready" stance).

Once you're up, take a minute to check a few
body parts. Are you crouched over? Getting low is the
goal, but only *from the waist down*. Keep your head up
and "sit up straight" with your upper body so your hips and shoulders are *stacked up* vertically.
In other words, don't let your butt poke out behind you. Instead, squeeze gently and tuck those
cheeks to keep them in line with your shoulders.

Also, bend those bolt-straight knees! Keeping your knees bent or *flexed* increases your range
of motion, lowers your center of gravity, and improves your balance. Think of Sheryl Swoopes or
Rebecca Lobo getting ready to sink a foul shot: Toes to the line, feet shoulder width apart, and
before that ball goes anywhere they pause with their knees bent and take a deep breath. Bingo!
Minus the ball and maybe a foot or two of height, that's your *ready stance*, too.

SIDESLIPPING PART 1: HEELSIDE

Once you're standing up, snowboarding is a little like riding a bike—it's actually much easier to
keep your balance if you're moving. The first step is to learn to slide down the slope with your
board turned sideways (so it goes slowly). Let's start with your heelside, since it tends to be easier, and, hey—you're already there.

Since you're already facing in the direction you want to travel, all it takes to get moving is
a little downward pressure with your toes. This part is just like stepping on the accelerator in a car,
except you make the same motion with both feet. Just press down ever so gently with the balls of

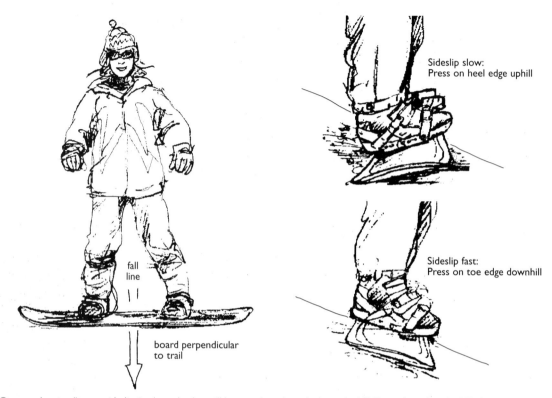

Sideslip slow:
Press on heel edge uphill

Sideslip fast:
Press on toe edge downhill

fall
line

board perpendicular
to trail

Once you're standing up, **sideslipping** is as simple as tilting your board gently down the hill. Flatten it against the hill more to accelerate (lower right), or dig the uphill edge to slow it down (upper right). "Remember, one edge at a time," says Betsy. "Also, think about keeping your weight equally distributed between both feet, 50–50."

your feet and toes, tilting your board down the hill. (Easy now; don't floor it.) This part of riding is always the same: Only your *uphill* edge touches the snow, since it can slide even with all your weight on it. Setting your *downhill* edge, however, is a lot like getting tripped: The edge will catch in the snow, stopping your feet while the rest of you tips over. Not to worry—as long as you are wearing knee pads and wrist guards, even tipping over is no big deal.

Okay, you're up and sliding. Be prepared as the board starts to move. Just as your body presses back against a car seat when you accelerate, it will naturally fall backward slightly as your board slides away down the hill. To compensate, lean forward equally slightly with your hips and upper body as you "hit the gas." A gentle tap requires no more than squeezing your abs in preparation. Going fast requires leaning much harder to keep your weight over the board. Take it nice and slow at first and get comfortable—you can always play with more speed later.

Troubleshooting

As you find your balance, a number of challenges can present themselves. Perhaps sideslipping just feels strange, since you've probably noticed that most of the time *the rider* faces sideways, while *the board* points down the mountain. Nice catch, but boards can pick up a lot of speed when you point them straight down the hill. The way to start is sideways, as that's how you go slowly and stop.

Or perhaps *steering* is the problem. Say your board keeps scooting off toward the trees, like a car veering off the highway. Most likely the board is not completely sideways (*perpendicular*) to the slope of the hill. To get your board perfectly sideways, start by pretending to drop an orange at your feet. Where it rolls is called the *fall line* of the hill. Like the current in a river, the fall line is the direction in which a mountain will naturally carry that orange, or you, or a person on a sled, or anything else that happens down it. You want your board directly *across*, or perpendicular, to that line. Start by orienting the board *before you stand up*, and then keep equal weight on both feet. As opposed to leaning one way or the other, keeping your weight centered between your feet will carry you straight ahead.

Speed can also be a challenge at this stage. Say you're slipping nicely along straight down the middle of the trail, but

• •

"**A** hundred bad habits can come from your upper body—breaking at the waist, counter-rotating, waving your arms—it's important to use your feet and knees, but also not to use your upper body in the wrong way. That was the biggest challenge for me—I had edging skills from skiing, but what actually got me linking turns was figuring out what to do with my upper body. It was like tennis—get the arms right, and the rest comes naturally. Keep your hands up and ready, like on the tabletop, and face in the direction that you want to go. That's what worked for me."

—Ali Napolitano

• •

moving a little too fast for comfort. As when you first stood up, remember to dig your edge into the snow by *flexing your feet* and *pressing your body weight down* into your heels. Doing this while stationary will hold the board still; doing it while moving will slow it down or even stop it. The more you pull your toes up, the harder your heels dig in, along with the edge underneath them.

Remember, though, it doesn't work if your knees are locked. Straightening your legs may be a natural and common response to fear, but exactly the opposite is necessary in snowboarding. The hairier things get, the lower you want to be. As mentioned earlier, bending or flexing lowers your center of gravity, improving your balance and forcing your weight down into your edge. This means your edges are, in effect, your brakes; and the fastest way to slam on them is to *push down* hard—which you can't do if your knees are locked. Train yourself to notice instantly when you get all locked up, and to react just as instantly with the opposite sequence of motions. This is the key to controlling your speed—your very own anti-lock brakes.

Finally, it's nice to wave at the people up on the chair, but keep in mind that it can knock you off balance. In other words, little wobbles here and there can get your arms waving and flailing faster than a highly caffeinated cheerleader. While this may prove entertaining for spectators, it only exacerbates balance problems for the rider. Keep your hands as quiet as possible, as if they're placed on that tabletop we discovered earlier.

Again:

- **Equal weight** on both feet and **board sideways** to steer straight ahead.

- **Flex** your feet and **drive your weight** into your edge to control speed.

- **Hands quiet** (as if on a tabletop) to avoid instability.

Each of these motions also will help to absorb any obstacles you come upon (though there won't be many, because beginner trails are carefully groomed for the express purpose of clearing these away). The worst you should see are a few snowbound versions of speed bumps and potholes. Trust your judgment, but keep in mind these things are made of snow. Unless it's icy, many will melt right out of your way. Take it slow at first, and you'll be surprised what you can manage.

Give yourself several chances to get a feel for sideslipping—and be prepared to tip over a few times. Everybody does. Even if your brain knows exactly what to do, it takes a little trial and error for your muscles to figure things out. Just try to learn something with every attempt, and be patient. It may well take half a run to feel your first flashes of progress, but "it's all downhill" from there.

FLIPPING OVER: THE SHOULDER ROLL

Sweet, you're sideslipping. Assuming that you're still on your heelside edge, you'll need to *flip over* to try the same thing on your toeside edge.

The easiest way to do this is to do a *shoulder roll*. Starting from a sitting position on your heelside (1), lie back and turn your body toward your rear shoulder (2). You want to lift the nose of your board up and over the

tail, so you wind up kneeling on your toeside edge. The hardest part is the first half, when you have to get the nose of your board up and over the tail (3). It's getting easier with all the super-light boards these days, but you may need your abs as well as your legs to get the board around. If necessary, it also helps to pull behind your front knee with your hand. Then just keep rolling toward that back shoulder, and your board will follow. As Betsy says, "try to make it one big move so you don't get stuck halfway, and keep your stomach muscles firm to avoid straining your back."

SIDESLIPPING PART TWO: TOESIDE

Once you're kneeling on your toeside edge, you're ready to stand up and sideslip. Getting up is refreshingly easy. Again, first be sure your board is *sideways* to the hill. Then just push yourself up with your hands. Keep the back hand down to steady yourself as you rise; reaching out with the other one for balance. As on your heelside, remember to rise until your shoulders and hips are *stacked up* in a line over your feet. It helps to tuck your butt under, keep your weight spread evenly over both feet, and to keep your hands at about waist level in front of you.

About the only difference between sideslipping on your toeside and heelside is what happens below the ankle. Here everything is opposite: All of your weight is on your toes, so balancing is a lot like standing on tiptoe. (Think of it like walking up a staircase covered with thick, pile carpet. Halfway up you realize you forgot something, and hesitate. Your front toes sink deeply into the carpet, stopping you, and your heel hangs in midair. Sinking down into your toeside edge is a similar sensation. It's as if both feet were there on the stair, with your toes digging into the carpet and your heels hanging in midair.) Pressing down into your toes is how you dig your edge in, slow down, and stop; easing up ever so gently allows you to go slipping down the hill.

Sideslipping toeside may come pretty naturally because most of us are used to balancing on our toes. It may also seem a bit awkward, however, since you're looking *up* the hill while sliding *down* it. If you find this disconcerting, *know the terrain below* for confidence. That is, take a good look at the snow on the trail below you before you actually stand up. Make note of any changes or obstacles there so they won't surprise you later. Also be aware of any people nearby and note which way they are heading.

Keep the movements subtle, and remember that flattening out your feet doesn't actually mean touching your heels to the ground: You still want your weight exclusively on your *uphill* edge (in this case your toeside), which slides even with weight on it. As discussed earlier, catching your *downhill* edge (in this case your heelside) will likely knock you over.

Finally, watch out for a tendency to look down at your feet. If you're with a riding buddy, have them follow you so you can look each other in the eyes. If you don't have one handy, now's your chance to resuscitate one of those imaginary friends from childhood, or to make friends with an intriguing stranger. (Go ahead—you can blame it on me.)

It's all pretty intuitive once you get there, and takes about as long as reading about it. Plan to give yourself a bunch of tries just in case, and build speed in small increments. Push it a little and stop, then a little harder and stop again. Pretty soon you'll be slipping smoothly at a variety of speeds.

PLAYING WITH STEERING: THE ZIGZAG

Once you're comfortable sideslipping down the centerline of the highway, it's time to change lanes. Looking down the trail from the top of the hill, you want to cross back and forth like a car

THE ZIGZAG

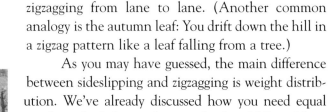

zigzagging from lane to lane. (Another common analogy is the autumn leaf: You drift down the hill in a zigzag pattern like a leaf falling from a tree.)

As you may have guessed, the main difference between sideslipping and zigzagging is weight distribution. We've already discussed how you need equal weight on both feet to slip straight ahead (1), and how the board needs to be sideways (or perpendicular) to the fall line. Zigzagging is kind of the opposite: You want to travel *across* the hill instead of *down* the fall line, which requires you to shift your weight in the desired direction. In other words, if you want to go *right*, shift some extra weight to your *right foot* (2, 3); if you want to go *left*, lean on your *left foot* (4). The board will respond by crossing, or *traversing* the hill in the indicated direction, whether you are standing toeside or heelside.

Shifting as little as 10 percent of your body weight can be all you need to change direction, so keep your movements subtle at first. If your board doesn't seem to respond, lean a little harder and "give it some gas."

Finally, something about focusing on your destination can help the rest come automatically. It helps to pick a target to aim for, like a tree or some other landmark at the side of the trail.

Take it slowly at first and do a few runs on each side. The first few tries can be downright awkward, but it all comes pretty quickly. Soon you'll be able to keep your balance, control your speed, and steer all at once. Then it's time to add a little juice, and keep at it until you can cross back and forth across the trail smoothly. Be sure you can do this equally well on both your heel- and toeside edges before moving on.

HEELSIDE TURN

STOP THAT! YOUR FIRST TURNS

The biggest challenge involved in your first turns is the mental commitment to see them through. First you go from a dead stop to pointing your board down the fall line (1, 2), which isn't so bad because you already know a bit about steering from zigzagging. Then there's a split second in the middle when you're picking up speed and have to change edges (3). This part will be new to you, and complicated by the rush of a little speed. The trick is to focus on *stopping* as soon as you reach this point (4, 5), which won't be too difficult if the words "Stop! Stop!" are already echoing in your mind. The best part is, you already know how.

Let's back up a little. Say you've been zigzagging back and forth and it's going pretty smoothly. You're even getting comfortable with speed, and oh, look, there's a nice flat section of trail ahead. You've decided you're ready to try a turn, but how?

Let's start with which way you're facing. Assuming you're stopped with the board across the hill, your bellybutton is either facing up the hill (toeside) or down toward the parking lot (heelside). In either case, the point is to wind up facing in the opposite direction.

TOESIDE TURN

To get there, weight your front foot and give the board some gas, just as you would to start a zigzag (1). This time you'll need to be a little more aggressive, pressing down long and hard enough to point the nose of the board straight down the hill (2). Then it's time to roll to your other edge. If you started on your toeside, for example, let the board flatten completely and transfer your weight to your heels. If you started on your heelside, roll from your heels to your toes (3). Then stop on the other side, just like you did when you were sideslipping . . . Remember? Turn the board sideways so it's across the fall line (4), tilt it so the uphill edge digs in, and get low to put more pressure on your edge (5). Again, it doesn't work if your knees are bolt straight so think anti-lock brakes.

There. *Point* the board down the hill, *roll* to your other edge, and *stop*. Congratulations—I think you just made your first turn.

Now try it on the other side, then link a few together. Keep stopping at the end of every turn so you don't carry speed from one turn to the next. Then add juice a little at a time, and pretty soon you won't have to stop at all.

Chapter 4

ESSENTIAL SKILLS

Photo by Ian MacKenzie; Rider: Betsy Shaw

Once you're out there making turns, progress is largely a matter of trouble-shooting. Some people have an incredible knack for staying balanced over their board but can't seem to get an edge into the snow. Others are quite comfortable with edging, maybe because of some ski-ing experience, but find the sensation of standing sideways takes some getting used to. Still others are complete naturals with everything related to technique but suffer the major wobbles for lack of snug boots and bindings.

These and other typical problems faced by beginners can be related to one of three fundamental skills: balance, edg-ing, and equipment awareness. The fol-lowing sections give detailed descriptions

"Drills are something you can keep coming back to—regardless of your ability level, they always help. Even if you're shy or self-conscious, find a place that's out of the way and not under a lift to practice. You can always do things at a different level later on—different intensity, faster—and it's going to keep on helping. It's not like you just learn how to snow-board and you're done. You're always learning, always getting better, and the fundamentals will always help."

—Ali Napolitano

of each of these skills, along with the problems associated with each and suggested exercises for improvement. Each exercise was selected based on its proven effectiveness in helping other women learn to ride comfortably and quickly. Start with the section that seems to be the weakest for you, and progress should be a few simple exercises away. Or, take a stab and start anywhere. The more you do, the faster you'll go from survival mode to smooth, solid riding. Just promise to take it slow and play around with each exercise long enough to feel a difference. Good luck!

BALANCE

Goal: Dynamic Balance	Typical Problems	Suggested Drills
• Get centered	• Hunching, stooping, looking down at your feet	• Twist versus resist (page 59)
• Get firm	• Arms/upper body flailing	• The Fonda squeeze (page 60)
• Get stacked	• Poking your butt out	• Vogue (page 61)
• Get low	• Jerky edge sets or "wobbles"	• Hands behind your back (page 63)
	• Tipping over (falling uphill)	• Donuts (page 64)
	• Catching an edge (falling downhill)	

The goal of dynamic balance

It's one thing to balance standing still, as on your tiptoes or holding one foot. Add the element of movement, like walking, riding a bike, or sliding on ice, and things get a little more complicated. Not necessarily more difficult, mind you (unless you're a whole lot better than I am at standing on one foot), but definitely different. Hence the concept of *dynamic balance*, or stability in motion.

Sounds pretty fancy, but if you're comfortable with any of those activities (walking, riding a bike, or sliding on ice), then you've already got a feel for dynamic balance. Consider riding a bike: Push off so you're moving forward and it's actually pretty easy to stay balanced side-to-side. You have to lean forward ever so slightly to keep your body over the moving bike, but other than that you can pretty much coast. Of course, you also have to keep an eye out for obstacles, lean into the turns, hunker down for the bumps, and so on. Scary stuff at first, but soon it becomes second nature. Soon it's bye bye training wheels, hello speed rush. Even little curb jumps start to look like fun.

Snowboarding is amazingly similar: You have to stay balanced over the middle of your board, yet you're always throwing your weight around. The hard part at first is not tipping over (just like on a bike), but that sense comes quickly. Once you get moving it's actually quite easy to coast along. Soon it's second nature, in fact, and then comes the good stuff—learning to throw your weight around, like the biker leaning into tight turns and hunkering down for the bumps.

Soon it's bye bye beginner runs, hello speed rush. Like Claire Dickerson, a 47-year-old law professor from Rye, New York, in a few short weeks you too may find yourself launching off the biggest hit in the park.

The keys to better balance

Get centered

Better balance is all in your center. Not to be confused with the midpoint of your board, *your* center (or center of gravity) is somewhere in your lower belly. Its specific location may vary depending on your body type, but let's just say it's somewhere behind your bellybutton and serves as a pivot point for your whole body. If someone were to tilt you on your stomach and spin you like a basketball, your center would be the spot that you'd be turning around. In a standing position it's also the point around which you'd spin sideways, like a figure skater or the little ballerina in a music box. Finally, it's also the point around which you would roll forward in a somersault, like a gymnast on the uneven bars. See what I mean? Everything revolves around your center.

Then there's the center of your board. Not to be confused with *your* center, the center of your board is just what it sounds like—the midpoint of the board from tip to tail and from side to side. There's no need to measure this or mark it on your board, but you do want to develop a feel for where it is. For now let's start with being aware that it's there, roughly halfway between your bindings, probably hidden under the stomp pad.

too far forward   centered   too far back

Line the two up, one over the other, and there's almost no knocking you over. You can resist all kinds of outside forces, like a weeble. (Remember those? "Weebles wobble but they don't fall down.") The bonus is that you can also *create* an impressive amount of force. It all comes from having *your* center lined up over the *board's* center, which—surprise—is called being *centered*.

Get firm

We've already touched on the keys to getting firm (remember your *ready stance* from Chapter 3), but here's a quick review: Getting *firm* means squeezing your abs and bum so little bumps can't throw you off balance. It's a little like getting punched in the stomach—firm up when you see it coming and the blow isn't as likely to send you flying. Make like the dough boy instead (soft in the middle) and it's a lot harder to control your board.

Get stacked

Step three toward better balance is getting *stacked*. Not to be confused with the plastic surgery alternative (this is going to be much better), getting stacked means standing in a position where your head, shoulders, hips, and ankles are lined up or *stacked* vertically. As we noted in Chapter 3, beginners have a tendency to bend over or stoop and let their bums poke out the back. A much stronger stance is to "sit up" with your head and shoulders, with your butt tucked under, so they all line up over your ankles. This way, gravity and other forces work *for* you instead of *against* you. (Think of it like carrying a child on your shoulders, a pack on your back, or doing squats at the gym: Keep your shoulders lined up over your hips and you can carry a fair amount of weight; get just a little bent over, however, and the same load will send you straight to the ground.)

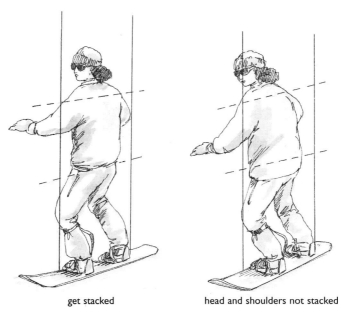

get stacked   head and shoulders not stacked

relaxed stance   get low

Get low

Getting *low* means using your knees to press your body weight *down into* your board. This drops your center of gravity and increases the pressure to your edges, making it much harder to tip over. As my friend Meghan "Geronimo" Giroux would say, "Be a bush, not a tree. Trees sway in the wind and are easy to knock down, but you don't see a lot of bushes that have fallen over." Just remember that stooping over and poking your butt out don't count—in fact, they make things much worse. Tuck your bum and use your knees to get low with your hips instead, like jumping out of bed, off a stair, or hunkering down for that bump on a bike.

Exercises: five steps toward better balance

Twist versus resist

Start by buckling into your board on a flat, even surface at the top of the bunny slope. (You'll need a perfectly flat surface so you can stand comfortably without moving.) Take a deep breath and relax completely, shaking your arms, legs, and booty to get good and loose.

Now, do the twist. Picture Richard Simmons, legs planted at about shoulder width apart, doing side twists in an exercise video. Or (in case you can't stand visualizing Richard Simmons) pretend that there's a big hairy monster standing directly behind you, and use only your upper body to turn for a look.

See how far you can get by turning with only your head, shoulders, and waist. You should be able to look almost directly behind you without moving your feet or your board. Turn the other way and back again, staying loose in your middle, and notice how easy it is to twist back and forth without ever moving your feet.

Now try the opposite: The monster is still directly behind you, but it's heinous and slimy and you can't stand to look. Resist the urge to sneak a peek by squeezing with your sides and belly so you can't turn your shoulders. Better yet, have a buddy stand behind you, grab your shoulders, and twist them, as if trying to turn your attention to whatever that thing is behind you. Again, resist by squeezing with your sides and belly so your shoulders can't budge. Notice how you have to use your cheeks (the bottom kind) to keep from being turned. Also note how as you firm up, any movement in your shoulders is transmitted to the board.

Alternate back and forth a few times to get a feel for the difference: Get all loose and twist both ways, and note how your board never moves. Then get good and firm, and see how the board moves with you. Aha! There's the feeling you're looking for—when the board moves with you because your midsection is firm.

Next, the trick is to take that feeling and apply it to your turns. With your new-found power belly nice and tight, make some turns down the bunny hill. After 10 or 15 turns, let your middle go loose again, so your arms and upper body twist all over the place. Make another 10 or 15 turns, and then firm up again with your sides and belly. You should notice a significant difference in how well the board moves with you, responding faster and more precisely to your "driving" as you firm up your midsection. Who'd have guessed, but there you have it—power steering in a simple squeeze.

The Fonda squeeze

Of course, squeezing your stomach is only half the battle—the top half. For the bottom part, start again by buckling in at the top of the bunny slope. Take a deep breath, relax, and stand comfortably still on your board.

With your knees slightly bent, tuck your butt under and squeeze your cheeks. This should feel pretty darn similar to the legendary Jane Fonda move, except of course that you're standing up.

Keeping your butt tucked under, rock back and forth a little from your toes to your heels and back again. Notice how tucking your bum under forces you to bend your knees more. (This may feel a bit wobbly at first, so take your time.) Keep at it until you can roll smoothly from your toes to your heels and back again without poking your butt out.

Again, the idea is to take this feeling and apply it to making turns. Go ahead and ride down the bunny slope, firmly tucking your bum back under whenever it pokes out. If your body position was already pretty good, you should notice an instant difference. If you have a tendency to bend over, however, you'll need to learn to use your feet and knees in new ways. Keep the focus at eye level (as opposed to looking down) and stick with it—your new turns will be worth it.

TOESIDE VOGUE

Vogue

As usual, start with a flat spot at the top of the beginner hill and buckle into your bindings.

Fold your hands behind your head like Madonna doing her *Vogue* routine, with your elbows straight out to the sides. Resist the tendency to let your back arch like someone trying to look all sexy, and keep your midsection firm instead.

Without moving your upper body, transfer your weight back and forth between your toes and heels. Notice how for stability you really have to use your knees and get low with your hips. If you have a tendency to lean in with your shoulders, having all that weight up high will magnify the wobbles. Again, squeeze your sides, belly, and bum to keep your elbows from dipping, and don't let yourself get bent over. You'll know when you hit the sweet spot because suddenly your body position feels infinitely more stable.

HEELSIDE VOGUE

Once you've got it standing still, take this position riding. It's a lot easier than it sounds so go for it, but start with a relatively flat section of trail so you won't have to worry about speed. Take it easy and make plenty of turns, stopping to regroup if you get discombobulated. Keep at it until you can "vogue" smoothly through both heelside and toe-side turns.

Hands behind your back

Like the previous exercise, riding with your hands behind your back forces you to use your lower body for balance. It's simple: Just rest the tops of your hands on your derriere and clasp your fingers together. (If you're wearing mittens or bulky gloves, just grab a thumb.)

The challenge is to take this position riding, without getting bent over or letting your bum poke out. By now the way to do this successfully is familiar: Choose a nice, flat section of trail and take it slowly at first so you can make adjustments without stressing about speed. It's important for all your later skills that you learn to steer your board with your feet, knees, and hips—not your upper body.

Donuts

Also known as 360s, donuts sound a lot scarier than they are. If you get at all intimidated think of Maureen O'Keefe, a 30-something camper from Women Only Snowboard Camps who laughed out loud at the thought of trying her first one. After all of three or four days snowboarding she was linking turns and able to control her speed on both green and blue runs. She was easily ready for some donuts, but of course she couldn't believe it. "You want me to do *what?*" she said. "No way!"

Yes, way. They're incredibly helpful, not that difficult, and anyone who can link a whole run of turns together smoothly is ready. (Which is what I said to Maureen after a quick demonstration. Three minutes later she was whirling down the trail so quickly that everyone else jumped in, and suddenly I was surrounded by spinning women. So take it from them: This is gonna be great.)

Again, start with a nice flat section of trail so you don't have to worry about speed. Taking it slow at first is doubly critical for this one, so think of it as if a 5 mph speed limit were suddenly in effect for the trail you're on. Repeat: *super slow.* Sounds boring, but it's a heck of a lot easier to learn that way—and you're less likely to smack in the process.

Standing on your heelside edge so you're looking down the mountain, choose a landmark well ahead of you to use as a target. This could be a tree, a trail sign at an intersection, or even the parking lot if it happens to be in sight. (Riding buddies are also good if you can get one to hold still for a while.)

Now *visualize* spinning 360 degrees. Start with a look at the nose of your board and visualize pointing it down the mountain at your target. Imagine spinning it in the same direction, until your back is facing the target, at which point you'll be standing on your toeside edge. (This part will feel quite familiar when you actually do it—it's just like a toeside sideslip.)

Donut motion

Below: Frontside donut (start facing down the mountain). **Right:** Backside donut (start with back facing down the mountain).

• •

"**W**hen I started I just loved snowboarding.
I was going down the steepest slopes
on the third day. It doesn't matter how
you look, you're going to get down
somehow—even if it's sideslipping, it
doesn't matter—it's how you get better."

—Christine Rauter, 25
Professional snowboard racer from Innsbruck, Austria

• •

Now comes the new part: Take a look at the tail of your board and point it down at the target, so you're essentially riding backward (don't worry, it only lasts for a second). Now you've only got 90 degrees to go, so keep turning until your bellybutton is facing down the mountain again.

Run through it a couple of times in your mind to get your bearings, and then it's time to go for it. The first half of the move is relatively easy: Weight your front foot to bring the nose of your board down into the fall line, just as you would to start a regular turn. Stop when you get to your toeside edge, which also will be quite familiar to you from your sideslipping practice.

The second half will feel a bit shakier, but the mechanics are the same: Weight your "front" foot (in this case actually your back one on the board because you are facing backwards) to bring the "nose" (in this case the tail) of your board down into the fall line. Then change edges by rolling smoothly from the balls of your feet to your heels, and slow down by bringing the board across the hill. At that point things will feel familiar again, since you're basically sideslipping on your heelside edge.

In most cases a moment of panic will strike during that first backwards edge change, but you already know what to do about that: Squeeze those abs and tuck your bum to keep the board underneath you, and it will respond by coming around faster. Then it's time for a high five, sister: You just completed your first 360.

Keep spinning in the same direction until you can get around smoothly, and then try turning the other way. This direction is usually slightly more awkward, so remember the rules for a backwards edge change:

- **Weight your back foot** to point the tail down the hill.
- **Roll smoothly** from one edge to the other.
- **Squeeze your middle** if you start to panic (no jelly belly here).
- **Bring the board across the hill** to slow down.

Finally, don't stop! Not that you'll want to because these are pretty fun, but they're also the ultimate snowboarding exercise. Take your time and learn to do them smoothly in both directions. Donuts do more than help your balance—they force you to learn how to use both your front and back legs, as well as the entire length of your board. I still do them all the time for a quick warm-up at the start of the day or to get a feel for a new board.

EDGING

• •

Goal: total edge confidence for steering, speed control

- Build *angles*
- Build *pressure*
- Build *early* in the turn

Typical Problems

- Lack of edge angle/no bite
- Too much edge angle/railing
- Pressure static/not enough
- Pressure too far forward (hip popped out to the side, over nose)

Suggested Drills

- Push-o-war (page 68)
- Hockey stops (page 69)
- Stomp the spider (page 70)
- Drive with your knees (page 71)
- Spank the crossover (page 73)
- Target turns (page 74)

• •

"**Y**our edges are your lifeline: The more you learn how to master them, the more control you will have over your board. The more control you have of your board, the wider the variety of trails you can feel comfortable on. Pretty soon there will be no place you can't go. Also, it is important to develop a feel for the snow. As conditions vary, so must your amount of edge pressure. The amount of edge pressure you need for hardpack or ice is much more than you need for soft snow or slush. It is important to learn to adapt to your particular environment—it's all part of mastering the mountain."

—Betsy Shaw

The goal of edging

There are two things you can do with your edges: *set* and *steer*. The steering part is pretty intuitive: You just point the nose of your board where you want to go and, by design, its edges will carry you there. Of course it gets a little more complicated than that—eventually you'll need to learn to steer through a variety of turn shapes and snow conditions, just as you would in a car. But basically, once you've actually learned to turn both right and left, the rest comes pretty naturally.

Setting your edges, on the other hand, can seem like a foreign concept at first. All it means essentially is digging your edge down into the snow, not by pointing the nose somewhere but by applying tilt or *edge angle* with your feet. By now you're quite familiar with this concept from learning how to sideslip and stop, but what about *while you're turning?* Sure enough, the same motion can be used at various points in a turn to create and carry speed, handle steep or icy conditions, or just carve for fun. It all depends on *where* and *when* you roll to your new edge in a turn: "early" in the turn (or at the top), when your board isn't quite down the fall line yet; in the middle, when it's pointing roughly straight down

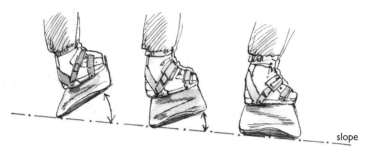

setting: angle of edge or base compared to slope

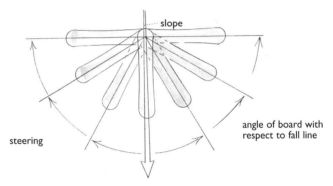

Essentially there are two things you can do with your edges: set and steer. **Setting** means using your feet to change the tilt or **edge angle** of your board relative to the slope of the hill. **Steering** means turning the length of your board so the nose points in the desired direction.

the hill; or "late" in the turn, when your board is already coming back across the hill.

As a beginner it's easiest to roll to your new edge at least halfway through the turn (when your board is already pointing down the fall line). Once you're comfortable at that point, however, it's time to think about rolling to your new edge *earlier,* or higher, in the turn.

Of course, much also depends on *how hard* you dig that edge into the snow. As a beginner it's tough to put much pressure on your edges, since you have to be both balanced and confident before you can really lean on your board. Once you have a little experience, however, getting pushy with your board will make it more responsive and fun. Again: Begin slowly but surely, Shirley. Then it's time to be more aggressive with the pressure you put on your edges.

early or top of turn

middle of turn

late or bottom of turn

carving = setting "early," or at the top of the turn, as opposed to waiting until the bottom half to dig in your edge

Get aggressive by pressuring your edges, which forces the board to bend into tighter, stronger turns.

Above: Betsy and Julia play push-o-war.
Facing page: Betsy demonstrates a toeside hockey stop.

"**N**o more squishy turns! This is a great way to slow it down and learn more control."

—Michelle Laboise, Warren, Vermont, on the push-o-war

Exercises: getting aggressive with your edges

Push-o-war

To get a feel for being aggressive with your edges while you're standing still, grab a riding buddy (or maybe a friendly stranger) at the top of the bunny slope.

Start by buckling into your board with your "opponent" facing you. You should be facing down the mountain with your buddy facing up. Be sure your buddy takes his or her back foot out of the binding for balance while you stay buckled in.

Grab each other's hands for balance and start pushing with your legs. The point is for your buddy to try and pull you down the slope while you resist. For you, this will mean *setting* or digging your edge in, as well as pushing hard against your board to keep it from moving. If this seems hard to visualize, think about your feet in a game of tug-o-war: *traction* is the name of the game. You have to *dig in* hard with your heels to keep that rope from slipping. The same goes for snowboarding: Your edge is your tread, so tilt your board up to put all your weight on it, dig in with your heels, and push with your legs for better traction.

Pull gently at first to get a feel for things, and then have your buddy pull a little harder. Don't let them tug so hard that you both go flying down the hill—you don't want to yank on each other—but increase the tension slowly so you can figure out how to resist more firmly. Watch for the tendency to poke your butt out; notice how you're actually much stronger if you tuck it under and keep your belly firm.

"**E**veryone has good and bad days, but the important thing is to stay positive. I've been so super-motivated lately. So many people look for other things, but it's all about making yourself happy, stoked, and motivated. You can't always win, you know? When things go bad, don't worry about it."

—Satu Jarvela
Professional rider from Helsinki, Finland

It also helps to keep your head up by looking at your opponent's face.

There—now that you're using both your back and legs to push against your board, you should be next to impossible to budge.

Hockey stops

Now let's work on a similar challenge, only this time you'll be moving. Again, pick a relatively flat, open trail for starters.

Begin by pointing your board straight down the hill and "letting it run" until you pick up some speed. Wait until you're pretty darn nervous, and then hit the brakes! That is, turn your board completely sideways and stop as fast as you can. This requires the same movements as the push-o-war: Tilt the board up so all your weight is on the edge, and dig in with your heels. Don't worry if you have a tendency to sit down on the first few tries—that's not unusual at first, and it takes a little practice to stop fast and keep your weight over the edge at the same time. Just remember to tuck your bum under and keep that midsection firm.

Next try the same thing on your toeside. Point your board down the hill (1) until you pick up a little speed (2), but this time turn it sideways and stop quickly on your toeside edge (3). This side takes a little more mental commitment, since you can't sit down to "chicken out," so make up your mind to see it through and start with a little less speed if necessary. Then add speed a little at a time, until you can ride and stop *fast* smoothly on both sides.

• •

"I feel so much more comfortable on steep terrain now. I've come a mile since this morning."

—Sue Denure, 39, mom and pharmacist from Lindsay, Ontario, after learning push-o-war and hockey stops

• •

EQUIPMENT AWARENESS

If you are having problems with either balance or edging, it's quite possible that a little equipment awareness will do wonders for your riding. Consider Ana Camargo, a self-described beginner, who, despite apparently perfect technique, was having a hard time getting her edges to dig into the snow. It just didn't make any sense until we tightened down her boots and bindings—and uncovered a strong intermediate who had been lost in loose footwear.

The moral of the story is to remember the following mental checklist: **WOBBLES SUCK**. Loosely translated, it goes like this: **WO**men's **B**oots and **B**indings that fit your feet must be **L**ined up over your **E**dges and **S**nug for smack-free snowboarding. If you are having balance or edging problems: **S**top, **U**nbuckle, **C**inch your boots a little tighter, and **K**rank down a notch on the boot or binding straps. In other words, make sure your feet are **SUCK**ed flat against the board! If your feet are swimming around, chances are that you will be as well.

I know it's a little messy, but hopefully it's also just what comes to mind should you wind up out there on your derriere one too many times. There are also a hundred other ways in which a little equipment savvy can make your life easier, but we'll get to those in the next chapters.

At mid-turn, "stomp the spider" to put more pressure on your edges and bend your board into a tighter turn.

Stomp the spider

Now that you can dig hard on both sides with your board sideways to the hill, it's time to think about doing the same thing in the middle of your turns. All it takes is leaning a little harder on either your toes or your heels, which increases the pressure on the respective edges. Again, pick a relatively flat trail to make it easier at first.

With apologies to anyone who happens to be fond of spiders, let's start with the idea that there's a big, hairy one lurking under your back heel (or, if you really love spiders, think *cockroach*). Go ahead and make a few turns as you normally would, except you want to stomp that spider every time you roll to your heelside edge. The sequence goes like this: Normal toeside, roll to your heelside, stomp the spider, back to your toeside. Remember, the spider is directly under your *heel only*. Just as you would on the kitchen floor, you have to flex your foot a little if you really want to squish it.

"**T**his feels better, like I have more control. I still don't feel smooth, but I sure feel better than I did an hour ago."

—Heather Leake, advertising executive from New Jersey, after doing edging drills

• •

"It takes some patience to learn. My first run I was in the ditch. I was pretty much crawling the whole way, so there's hope."

—Aurelie Sayres, Pro snowboarder, East Haddam, Connecticut

• •

At this point you will probably notice some new sensations, like maybe the board "shoots" you out of the turn a little faster than usual. That's the whole point, so keep at it, stomping only once per heelside turn, and note how the effect changes depending on when and how hard you stomp.

Now try the same thing toeside. Let's say the tarantula that was hiding under your heel is somehow getting away. In fact, it's running right up the sole of your back foot and heading toward your toes. Again, think about how you would squish it at home on the kitchen floor and go for the same feeling while standing on your board. Can you feel the difference in how your board responds? Bingo. Dead creepy-crawlies make for some pretty snappy turns.

Drive with your knees

It's easy to think about initiating turns with your arms, shoulders, or head, but what about with your lower body? Actually, it's much easier to create both *edge angles* and *pressure* by driving through turns with your knees.

Let's start with making a few turns normally, paying special attention to what you do with your knees. Are they locked together in the middle and basically facing each other? Or do you ride "stinky," with your knees wide apart and pointing in opposite directions? These are the extremes, while somewhere in the middle is optimum.

Right: Driving both knees toward an imaginary X off the nose of your board is a much stronger stance than pointing your knees together (**above left**) or riding "stinky" (**above right**).

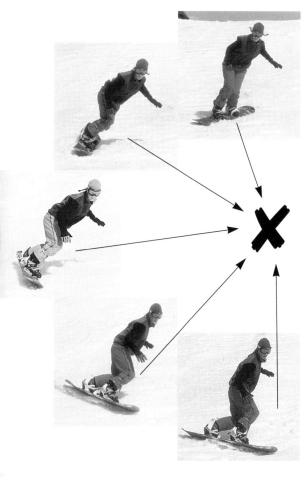

Take a look at the front half of your board, and picture a big X a few feet away from each side of the nose. Now, try standing still on each edge with your knees pointing at those Xs. This part is easier with a buddy to lean on (or any handy stationary object that will support you, like a bench, fence, trail sign, or even the base lodge). Try your toeside first as it's usually easier. Start by rolling up onto your toeside edge and pointing both knees at the X off the toeside tip of your board. Then drive or push your knees forward in that direction, using your hips and upper body to follow through with the motion.

Heelsides can seem slightly more awkward (since your knees don't bend that way), but the idea is the same: As you change edges and transfer your weight to your heels, picture both your front and back knees pointing at the X off your heelside edge. Then go ahead and drive them toward it. Get a little extra push by using the sides of your feet (the outside of your front foot, the inside of your back one), and by squeezing your back cheek. Sounds a little goofy, I know, but wait until you see the turns this makes.

Once you've tried this standing still, put the exercise in motion by driving your knees through each turn. (It also can help to picture the Xs as a foot tall and standing up, in which case your objective is actually to drive *through* them with your knees.) Be prepared to have your board snap around in new ways, which will make you look like a hero as soon as you get used to it. It won't take long; just squeeze with your abs to keep things together and remember to do the Fonda squeeze as you move through the turn.

Finally, try moving the Xs back and forth now and then to vary the shape of your turns. Placing them farther away from the board will make your turns round and tight, and relatively slow; placing them closer to your board, however, should take you straight and fast.

Spank the crossover

Another key to good turns is to start them early. This means rolling to your new edge sooner.

Start by thinking about what you normally do between turns, in the *crossover* or *transition* from heelside to toeside and vice versa: Your board is probably fairly sideways to the hill as you exit the first turn, and it stays flat on the snow for a long time before you roll to your new edge. *Spanking the crossover*, however, means minimizing the transition time from one edge to the other.

Again, start with a relatively flat section of trail so you don't have to worry about controlling your speed. Make a few turns, taking note of your timing as you exit each one. When exactly do you roll off of one edge and onto the next? What happens in between? It may actually help to count: 1) when you decide to finish the first turn and start rolling off your edge (either toeside or heelside); 2) when your base is flat on the snow but you haven't engaged the new edge yet; and 3) when you roll to your new edge, beginning a turn in the other direction.

Now let's think about rushing the process. As you finish the first turn (1), think about slapping your board down quickly so the base is flat on the snow (2). Then you'll be set up to roll to your new edge right away (3), while the nose of the board is still pointing away from you (as opposed to down the fall line).

At first you may notice it takes a while to get out of the first turn because your hips and upper body have to catch up with your board. Try pulling your feet and legs *up the hill* underneath you to make it go faster. Then be ready with that new edge (and, of course, to repeat the process as soon as your board comes around again). Also, get ready for a little speed rush! Setting your new edge early in the turn is both a way to *accelerate* and to *carry speed* effectively from turn to turn.

Mastering target turns is an essential prerequisite to catching air, when full-speed landings necessitate speed control. **Here:** Author Julia Carlson rides for a VISA commerical at Killington, Vermont.

Target turns

Of course, once you start accelerating, it also helps to know how to control speed. You already know how to bail out and stop, but what if you just want to slow down while turning? That's when short, braking turns come in handy. These entail scrubbing just a little speed with every turn as opposed to stopping altogether.

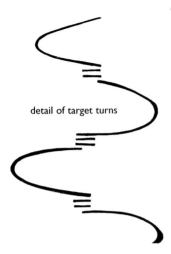

detail of target turns

Turn board completely sideways and sideslip between each turn to decrease speed.

This is one exercise you might want to do on a slope with some pitch to it. Start by picking a target dead ahead and way down the trail so you have room to do lots of turns before you actually get there. Take a guess at how many turns it would normally take you to get there and then double the number that comes to mind.

Aiming straight for your target, pack in as many tight little turns as you possibly can between your start and finish points—you'll have to be quick going from edge to edge—then push your board into a sideslip with each turn to scrub speed. Think of doing hockey stops, except you never want to come to a complete stop between turns.

It may take some time to get a feel for target turns, but consider this: Once you can be quick from edge to edge *and* control your speed, you're ready for more challenging terrain. Take it up a notch at a time and pretty soon you should be enjoying even the steepest trails.

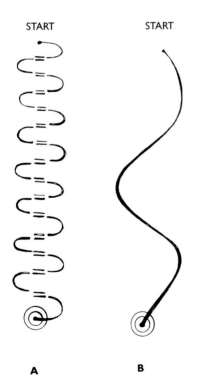

START   START

A   B

Target turns: Do fifteen short turns (A) where you would normally do three or four long ones (B). It helps to turn your board completely sideways and sideslip; this scrubs some speed at the end of each turn (see detail above).

Chapter 5

BUYER'S GUIDE TO GEAR

Photo by Dan Hudson; Rider: Karleen Jeffery

First and foremost, what you buy for snowboarding equipment depends on what you want to do with it. In many cases, gear is designed for a specific purpose: launching airs in the halfpipe, carving turns on groomed slopes, surfing three feet of fresh powder, and so on. No single setup will do everything well, so it's important to have some idea of where and how you'd like to begin—you'll want to buy equipment to match.

CHOOSING YOUR STYLE

Freestyle

The main attraction of *freestyle riding* is the rush that comes from time in the air. In the beginning this may be as simple as learning to pump the walls of a halfpipe or to hit a straight jump just big enough to get you off the ground. Pretty soon you're an adrenaline slave, drawn time and again to the pipe and park in search of bigger air and new tricks.

At its finest, freestyle is pros like 31-year-old Morgan Lafonte launching a back flip 35 feet off the ground; CaraBeth Burnside grinding a picnic bench and ruling the pipe with her feline, skate-style moves; and Shannon Dunn spinning huge 540s to win a bronze medal in the halfpipe at Nagano. If what inspires you most about snowboarding is getting off the ground with style, then you'll probably want to focus on freestyle.

Freeriding

Freeriding is more of a "soul" sport, dedicated to exploring terrain all over the mountain. First you learn to float in fresh powder, try some bumps, or venture off the beaten path for a run in the woods. Soon you're a powder hound, searching far and wide for deeper snow and fresh tracks. At its best, freeriding is pros like Karleen Jeffery, winner of the Alaskan "Queen of the Hill" World Extreme Championship, navigating a peak so steep and remote they haven't even named it yet; or sister Canadian Jennie McDonald, a backcountry guide-in-training, hiking and heli-boarding untouched snowfields all winter in the Rockies of British Columbia. If you have a similar taste for adventures in untracked powder, you'll probably want to focus on freeriding, as well.

Alpine or carving

Carving is the art of making turns that are graceful, fluid, and, above all, powerful. In the beginning, this can be as simple as learning to keep your board on edge all the time or learning to "let it run" at full speed on a relatively flat trail. Pretty soon you're a speed fiend, arcing turns back and forth across freshly groomed slopes where the snow looks like giant corduroy. At its finest, carving is pros like Betsy Shaw, 1996 World Giant Slalom Champion and 10-year veteran of the Women's World Pro Tour, rocketing down mile-high mountains in 60 seconds or less; or Alaskan Rosey Fletcher, teeth bared to reveal the diamond twinkling in her front tooth, braving blinding spring fog to win the U. S. Open Super G Championships. If what inspires you most about snowboarding is slicing smooth and solid turns the way these ladies do, you'll probably want to focus on carving.

Of course the styles blend at times, and so does the equipment. Good freestylers carve between jumps to control their speed and line up for the next hit; good freeriders boost airs with style and carve turns between tight trees; and good racers pop off knolls or turn and carve in reverse from time to time. Overall champs Michele Taggart, Victoria Jealouse, and up-and-comer Leslee Olson have each made names for themselves for their ability to "do it all." If what you really crave is a little taste of everything, don't worry—they make stuff for that, too.

BOARDS

As you might have guessed by now, snowboard gear falls into the same three categories. Different boards, boots, and bindings will perform very differently on the mountain, so it's important to consider the respective merits of each category before making a purchase.

Basic shapes

The easiest way to tell boards apart at first is by their shape. Just like people, boards come in a variety of lengths, widths, nose and tail profiles, and other easily recognizable features.

Different boards have different tail and nose profiles. Freestyle boards have turned-up noses and tails for easy riding forward and backward (switch). Freeriding boards have longer noses for better float in powder. Alpine boards have smaller noses and squared-off tails for a more powerful turn exit.

Freestyle

Generally, freestyle boards tend to be short and wide, which makes them ideal for riding in the pipe or park. The short length makes them light and easy to maneuver; the extra width provides lateral stability and a solid platform for taking off and landing airs. It also allows you to stand facing directly sideways on the board, which makes riding backward or "switch" as comfy as riding forward.

Freestyle boards also tend to feature relatively blunt nose and tail profiles. Boards curve up off the snow in front, just like sleds and skis, so you won't trip or get stopped in your tracks by bumps and other obstacles. Freestyle boards also curve up in the back for easy switch riding. These curved ends, called the "tip" or "nose" (in front) and the "tail" (at the back), are fairly small on freestyle boards. This helps keeps the board light, maneuverable, and easy to spin, whereas bigger noses and tails are heavier and more cumbersome.

Freestyle boards also have some limitations. The fact that they are shorter makes them

Freestyle boards are relatively short and wide for easy riding in the pipe and park. **Here:** Racer Kim Stacey shows the crowd at the U.S. Open that she also knows how to use a freestyle board.

less stable at high speeds, so they start to rattle around as you pick up speed on the ground. Also, wider boards take longer to move from edge to edge between turns. Finally, small noses tend to sink in fresh or deep snow (as opposed to "floating" above the surface), which makes it hard to ride powder.

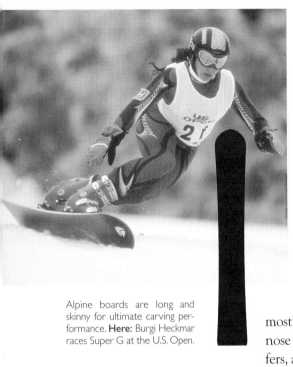

Alpine boards are long and skinny for ultimate carving performance. **Here:** Burgi Heckmar races Super G at the U.S. Open.

Alpine

Alpine boards fall at the opposite end of the shape spectrum: They are relatively long and skinny, which makes them ideal for high-speed carving. The extra edge ("running length") provides stability at speed, while narrowness makes them super quick from edge to edge. This shape also allows you to ride a "steep" stance, with your feet and body angled forward toward the nose of the board. This stance is ideal for carving because it allows you to align your knees over the edge in both heel- and toeside turns.

Alpine boards also tend to feature even smaller nose and tail profiles than freestyle boards. Since they are not generally used in bumpy or variable terrain, they don't need big noses for terrain clearance. Also, since they are not generally used to ride backward very often, most don't flare up off the snow much in the tail. Instead, the nose on most alpine boards is short and low for quick edge transfers, and the tail is long and flat for a more powerful turn finish.

On the downside, alpine boards won't float in powder well because of the small nose, and the flat tail makes them difficult to ride backwards. All that extra length can make alpine boards heavy and hard to lift or spin. Finally, narrowness makes them sink in powder and means they will be less stable laterally for takeoffs and landings.

Freeriding

In between freestyle and alpine shapes are freeriding boards of moderate length and width. These offer the best of both worlds for all-mountain performance. A good freeriding board is just long and narrow enough to carve fairly well, yet still short and wide enough to be fun in the air. The moderate width also allows for a moderate stance, which means your feet are not directly sideways or angled way forward. Instead, they sit about halfway between for a combination of carving and freestyle performance.

Freeriding boards of moderate length and width offer all-terrain performance. **Here:** Freerider Karleen Jeffery gives new meaning to the phrase "all terrain."
(Photo by Dan Hudson)

Freeriding boards also tend to feature longer, rounder noses than either alpine or freestyle boards. This provides clearance for the broad variety of freeriding terrain and snow conditions, which can change drastically from day to day and from mountain to mountain. For example, a nose that is very long and high will float extremely well in 3 feet of fresh powder.

On the downside, freeriding boards are more versatile than their alpine and freestyle cousins, but they won't carve or fly quite as well. They're a little too long to spin as effortlessly or tweak in the halfpipe, and a little too wide to carve quite as easily as a full-on racing board.

Sizing and fit

Length

Just as clothes range from extra small to extra large, most board "shapes" or "models" are also available in a variety of sizes. The difference is that boards are sized by *overall length,* which is measured in centimeters from the tip to the tail of the board. Freestyle boards tend to be the shortest at 140 to 155 cm for most women; freeriding boards are slightly longer at about 145 to 160 cm; and alpine boards are longer still at 150 to 165 cm.

Within each category, determining the length that's right for you depends on your height, weight, and ability level. The height part is fairly straightforward: A munchkin like me (at 5-foot-zip) would start with the shortest option in any given category (140 for freestyle, 145 for freeriding, or 150 for alpine), while Cheryl Swoopes or Rebecca Lobo would start at the long end, and a woman of average size would start in the middle.

Then, it's important to adjust your board length up or down if your weight varies considerably from the average. Larger riders need a bigger platform for stability, while flyweights need less board to push around. Should I swallow a watermelon and gain 15 pounds tomorrow, for example, I'd switch up from the 140 cm freestyle to about a 145 cm. Should I suddenly drop 15 pounds instead (ya, right) I'd have to go down a size to get the same control.

It's also important to bump up or down according to your ability level. Experienced and aggressive riders can handle a lot more board than beginners, who have an easier time learning

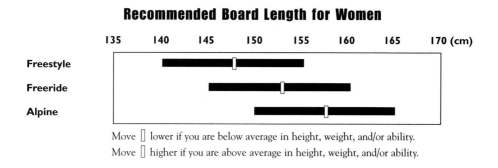

Recommended Board Length for Women

Move [] lower if you are below average in height, weight, and/or ability.
Move [] higher if you are above average in height, weight, and/or ability.

when there's a little less board to push around. Hence world-cup rider Tricia Burnes chooses "the longest board [she] can find that's narrow enough," while beginners are better off going down 5 cm for those first few days on snow.

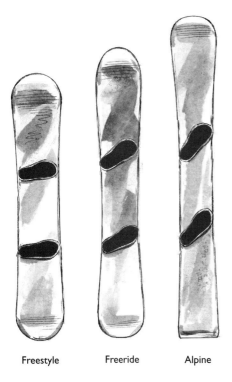

Freestyle   Freeride   Alpine

Width

An equally critical measurement is *board width*. Recall the necessity of having a board as wide as your feet are long for optimum balance and leverage. This means people with smaller feet need narrower boards, while those with bigger dogs need to go wider.

The right width also is a function of stance angles: Freestyle boards are meant to be ridden with your body facing sideways (feet straight across the board—therefore maximum width); freeriding boards with your body facing somewhat toward the nose (feet angled forward 15 to 30 degrees—therefore a slightly narrower board); and alpine boards with your body facing almost directly forward (feet angled 45 degrees or more—therefore a still narrower board).

Specific numbers can be hard to come by, but most women ride boards 18 to 25 cm wide at the waist. Again, freestyle models are at the wide end of the spectrum at 23 to 25 cm for most women. Freeriding boards traditionally have featured about the same waist widths in longer lengths (making them only *proportionately narrower*), though newer models are starting to go below the 23 cm threshold. Finally, alpine boards are the narrowest at roughly 18 to 21 cm.

If you're a tech betty and into board specs, use your shoe size and the ranges listed above to target a specific width in any given board category. Another approach is to try standing on various boards for comparison: Lay the board flat on the ground and stand on it, feet about shoulder width apart and angled according to the type of board you're trying. Then you can pretty much eyeball it to see if your toes and heels line up over the edges. Don't let the fact that snowboard boots can be bulkier than street shoes sway you—the whole point is to have your toes and heels lined up over the edges, and most bindings will raise you off the board enough to compensate for boot bulk.

Otherwise, it generally comes down to requesting a board that's somewhere between "extremely narrow" and "wide for a woman," depending on your shoe size. In this case, be sure your sales help is truly familiar with the needs of female feet, and remember: Balance is everything. Don't buy a board until you're confident that it's going to fit your feet once you're all mounted up.

Flex

The third big issue when it comes to fit is a board's *flex*, or how much it's going to bend when you ride it. This is a tough one to gauge in the shop because nobody likes newton-meters, which is how the engineers measure it. Instead, boards are generally categorized as simply "soft" or "stiff." This is fine, but understand it's also a little simplistic: It doesn't quite do justice to the varying degrees of flex, which can be extremely soft, moderately soft, medium, somewhat stiff, very stiff, incredibly stiff, and so on. It also doesn't reflect the fact that flex

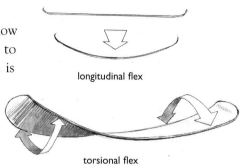

longitudinal flex

torsional flex

changes over the length of a board: Most feature a *directional* flex pattern—moderately flexible in the nose for easy bending into turns and slightly stiffer in the tail for a more powerful turn release. (The major exception is a *twin tip* freestyle board, which features the same flex pattern in the tip and tail for comparable performance riding forward and switch.) Finally, "soft" and "stiff" don't quite describe *torsional flex*, or the extent to which a board will *twist* in opposite directions at the tip and tail. Torsionally stiff boards provide superior edge grip and response, whereas torsionally soft boards will twist and slide off their edges.

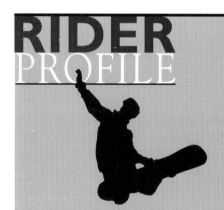

RIDER PROFILE

STACIE GENCHI
Founder and co-owner of
On Edge Girl's Board Shop
in Huntington Beach, California

Age: 31
Height: 5'2"
Weight: 112
Foot Size: 4½–5
Years Riding: 8

The philosophy behind On Edge is "not to exclude guys," says Stacie, but certainly "to cater to women. We're kind of the opposite of everyone else—90 percent women's stuff, 10 percent guys', and we do have guys who shop here." On Edge is also the home of Operation NBD (as in "Never Been Done"), an innovative learn-to-ride program. Armed with a vision of low-cost, accessible snowboard lessons for otherwise intimidated female never-evers, On Edge went to the SIA (Snow Sports Industries America) for help. The result was a start-up grant and a weekend program with gear rentals, transportation, lift tickets, and three days of women-only snowboard lessons for $225. Bombshell Clothing, makers of women's snowboard outerwear since way back when, even kicked in some loaner clothes. *(continued next page)*

RIDER
PROFILE
CONTINUED

EQUIPMENT ◄-------------◄--------------◄----------

"I ride a Goddess 145. I tried their boards and really liked them because they don't chatter. They're stiffer or less forgiving than most women's boards, which makes them hold an edge better. I liked that a lot. It's also really narrow, which is good because I have such small feet. I'm also into the girl thing—supporting a company that's doing exclusively women's boards, and Goddess was one of the first.

"I ride Goddess bindings, too. They're your basic two-strap freestyle binding, except both straps have ratchets for easy in/easy out. People ask me why I don't ride step-ins, and the answer is because I don't need them. They are too heavy for me anyway, and they hurt my knees, but, like I said, my ratchets are so fast that I just don't need them. I've never had the feeling that I didn't get enough runs in because my bindings aren't as fast as step-ins. And it doesn't bug me to sit down because I don't have to—I just bend down to buckle. Having a ratchet on both the ankle and toe straps makes it fast and easy, plus mine are big, which is nice, since gloves are always too big."

BOOTS ◄-------------◄--------------◄----------

"I ride N boots from Northwave. It's an all-around model, two years old, and I love them. I used to get incredible heel lift, and I tried everything to fix it. The guys told me to put more socks on, so there I was, riding around in two or three pairs of socks. I'd start with nylons— which just make everything slippery—it was awful. Then I tried straps, custom heel pockets—everything. Because my feet are so small, I have to put a lot of pressure on my toes and heels to get the board on edge. So my heels would always lift—until I got these boots. They're really cushy on the inside and have a good heel cup, so my heel doesn't lift at all. Nowadays I'm just really stoked. I wear one pair of the thinnest socks possible, tie up my boots and don't even worry about it. They're perfect."

Put all that back together and flex affects ease of turning, directional stability, vibration, damping, and plain old fun. Boards with stiff flex patterns take more muscle to bend into a turn, but they'll slice through all the bumps and crud you run into as snow conditions vary. They're also less likely to vibrate (so you get a smooth ride at high speeds), and torsionally stiff boards provide superior edge grip.

Meanwhile, boards with soft flex patterns are just the opposite: easy to bend into a turn, but more likely to bend around bumps and objects. They are also more likely to chatter as you pick up speed, and torsionally soft boards can "peel off," or slide, when you want them to hold an edge.

To find the flex pattern that's right for you, consider your weight, strength, and ability level, as well as your performance preferences. Heavy, strong, and aggressive riders need stiffer boards; smaller, lighter riders and beginners tend to need softer ones. (Note that "soft" is a relative term, and one that has traditionally been blown out of proportion for women. It's important to be clear about your weight, strength, and ability level, and to communicate this information matter-of-factly to salespeople.) Keep in mind that practically no one is a beginner after the first three days, so *rent* a soft board, but don't buy one. Also, don't underestimate how fast you'll learn. Most people are surprised at their progress—you don't want to outgrow a board before you're finished paying for it.

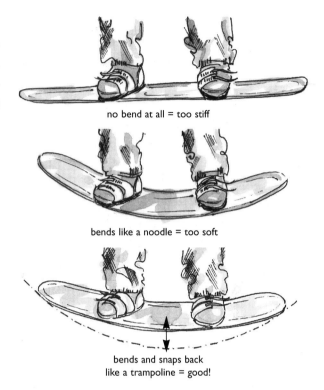

no bend at all = too stiff

bends like a noodle = too soft

bends and snaps back
like a trampoline = good!

The goal is to find a board that's soft enough to bend into turns yet stiff enough to snap back a little—like the rebound in a trampoline. A board that's as soft as a wet noodle will have you doing somersaults and sliding on your butt; one that's too stiff is like trying to ride a picnic table. Get some trustworthy help on this one if you need it and strike a balance for control and excitement.

Price points

Apart from coming in a range of shapes and sizes, boards are made for a variety of budgets. Some use the most sophisticated possible features and materials, promising to deliver the ultimate performance at a cost of $400 to $500. Others offer more moderate performance, usually at a savings of $100 to $200, and still others are downright cheap in terms of both price and performance. A bare-bones knowledge of construction and materials can help you decide which is for you.

Construction

Traditional snowboard construction is called *sandwich:* The top and base are sheets of different types of plastic that seal everything inside, a little like the slices of bread that hold a sandwich together. In between is a slice of specially contoured wood or foam (or sometimes both) called the *core.* This core is protected above and below by super-tough sheets of fiberglass, and all the way around on the sides by an equally tough plastic "sidewall" crust. The mayo and mustard are fancy adhesives that bind everything together, aided by heat from special ovens ("molds") that cook the boards into shape. Finally, sharpened steel edges are built in around the base for gription in slippery snow.

A common variation on the sandwich is called *cap construction*. Like a sandwich with the crust cut off, cap boards eliminate the thick plastic sidewall by wrapping the topsheet and fiberglass down over the sides of the core. The resulting boards don't always look much different on the shelf, but they can ride quite differently. Cap boards tend to cut into the snow more, making them extremely responsive. (Some would say too responsive. It's totally a matter of personal preference, even the experts disagree.) Sandwich boards are more torsionally forgiving.

A *RIM* or "squirt" board can look exactly like a sandwich or cap board on the outside, but it is totally different on the inside. Instead of being put together by hand out of carefully contoured parts, RIM boards are injected with liquid foam at high speeds and pressures. This makes for a quick and cheap manufacturing process, but the resulting boards tend to not perform as well.

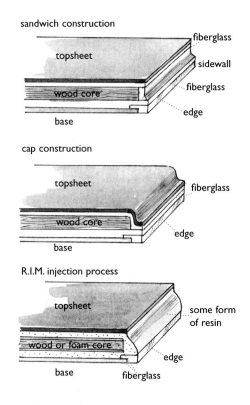

Materials

We have just discussed the basic list of snowboard ingredients: metal, plastic, fiberglass, wood or foam, and adhesives. It gets a little more complicated than that, of course, but the most important thing to realize about snowboard materials is that they all come in *varying grades*. If nothing else, recognize that "high-end" boards tend to use the lightest, strongest, most durable combination of materials to deliver optimum performance. They cost more, but the payoff is snappy response in a lightweight package, with fast and slippery base materials that won't scratch or dry out all the time. Meanwhile, "price-point" boards are made to be just that: inexpensive. You save money, but you also sacrifice in terms of weight, response, maintenance, and overall durability.

- **Bases** are made of ultra-high-molecular-weight (UHMW) polyethylene plastic, commonly referred to as "P-Tex" (though that's actually a brand name). UHMW comes in a variety of grades, which are numbered 1000-4000. Low-grade polyethylene tends to be *extruded*, a manufacturing process that results in bases that are relatively slow, easy to scratch or ding, and require frequent waxing. Higher grades are *sintered*, a longer and more expensive process that yields faster, more durable bases that hold wax longer. Super-duper but rare *electra* bases (recognizable because they're black) are even faster.

- **Core material** helps determine a board's flex and weight. Most cores are made of wood or foam, or sometimes both. Wood is "snappier" (or more responsive), holds its shape better, and can also be incredibly light. It's also more expensive. Foam is cheaper and can be lighter, but its soft and spongy nature tends to feel "dead" compared to wood, and it's not as durable. (When shopping, note that actual board weights are not generally advertised, which is why it's super important to toss a few around for a hands-on comparison.)

- **Fiberglass** is made from threads that are woven into sheets, like a rug or a kitchen placemat. Good boards use strong, clean weaves to increase strength and to help create a consistent and snappy flex pattern. Cheaper weaves can be messy and inconsistent, leading to boards with similar flex patterns and weak spots susceptible to breakage. The orientation of the glass is also important: Standard glass has two sets of strands woven perpendicular to each other ("biax" or "90 degree"); stronger glass has three sets of strands woven at 60-degree angles ("triax"), which makes the glass (and the resulting boards) stronger from corner to corner (torsionally stiffer). These boards resist twisting better, which means they will also hold an edge and *track* or steer better on the hill.

- **Edges** are made of steel, which also comes in varying grades. The harder the steel, the more your edges will resist impact damage and stay sharp between tunes. When shopping, note how some edges wrap up and around the tip and tail of the board, protecting against obstacles and wear and tear in liftlines, cars, and lunchtime crowds. Other edges stop where the board curves up off the snow, saving weight but potentially affecting durability.

Care of assembly

A quick top-to-bottom inspection of a board can tell you a lot about the quality of its construction.

1. Check the **topsheet.** Starting with the top, look for wrinkles or bubbles in the outer layer of plastic, called the topsheet. Also check for gaps or cracks around the holes (or "inserts") for the bindings, which should be flush with the topsheet.

2. Check the **sidewalls.** On the sides, check for cracks or discoloration, which can indicate a patch in the sidewall. Also, check the seam above each edge for cracks or separation from the base. (This goes for the ends of the board as well as the midsection.)

3. Check the **base**. It's easiest to check the base by holding it up to a light source: It should look wet (or waxy) as opposed to dry and "hairy," and you shouldn't see any weird indentations or bubbles under the binding inserts. Again, check the seam along each edge for gaps or separations.

4.   **Sight down the edge**. To do this, stand the board up on its tail and turn it sideways. Next, take a step back and pull the nose under your chin, closing one eye and sighting down the edge. It should form a nice clean curve from the nose to the tail of the board, without any kinks, wobbles, or distinct flat spots. Be sure to do this for both sides of the board, as they are "cooked" in the production process and can sometimes twist as they cool down.

If you notice problems with a particular deck, try checking out another one of the same model and size, just as you would with a piece of clothing. If that one also is flawed, it's probably best to go with a different brand.

Other board considerations

Women-specific boards

Do you need a women-specific board? Not necessarily. Certainly there are excellent options within this category, like the dozens of "signature models" designed specifically for pro riders like Shannon Dunn (Burton), Tina Basich (Sims), Morgan Lafonte (K2), Barrett Christy (Mervyn Manufacturing/Gnu), Jennie Waara (Ride), and so on. Also of note are non-signature lines for women, like Morrow Snowboards' Wildflower series (targeted at advanced women), and K2's Luna series, developed by marketing mavens Heidi McCoy and Hailey Martin.

On the other hand, plenty of so-called women's boards are nothing special except for the label, while plenty of unisex and even men's designs work great for women. The logic goes something like this: Board design is a function of overall rider profile, which includes height, weight, foot size, stance preference, ability level, riding style, and more. Put all those variables together and, as often as not, women and men of different sizes wind up happy on the same boards.

For example, pro rider Leslee Olson stands about 5-foot-11, weighs around 150 pounds, and has a women's size 11 foot. One of her favorite boards for freestyle is the Custom 155, which also happens to be a favorite of teammate Dave Downing (5-foot-9 or so, also about 150 pounds, with a men's size 9 foot). Another example is the popularity of Terje Haakonsen's signature model board with women. While Terje has dominated the men's tour for years, his stiff-but-narrow Balance design is a hit with both advanced women and guys with smaller feet. (Not to discriminate, it works the other way, too: Women's sig models have enjoyed similar success with guys. As shop owner Christine Pollio, of the B-Side in Burlington, Vermont, explains, "Board sales are pretty unisex. We sell a lot of women's pro models to boys as well as to women, but we don't have a lot of luck with women-specific boards.")

That may change as female participation rises and, of course, there's nothing wrong with liking the idea of boards made just for women. Just keep in mind that, as a shortcut for finding the right size and shape, "women's" doesn't tell the whole story—it's about finding the right length, width, flex, quality, and so on.

Graphics

One of the coolest things about snowboards is they're such a great canvas for artwork. There's a lot of empty space around the bindings on top, and the entire base practically begs for decoration. So what's a snowboard company to do about it?

Let's just say the answers to that question will probably surprise you. A few manufacturers simply take advantage of the billboard space with yet another corporate logo, but some pay entire teams of graphic artists and illustrators to go absolutely nuts with original designs. The results are as exciting, different, and hard to describe as any other art. Subjects range from clip-art classics like the Mona Lisa or the Muppets to tattoo art and nature photography à la Ansel Adams. A few particularly imaginative designs use the top and base to tell a story (like the one a few years back with a lonely, tied-up dog on top; on the base it's suddenly free and jumping to catch a Frisbee). Sometimes there's no subject at all, just "beautiful shapes and colors," as the designers say.

Pretty inspired stuff on the whole, with plenty of flavors to choose from. Just promise to focus on fit first, then decide on graphics.

Warranty

Most boards come with a warranty against defects for at least a year from the date of purchase. Be sure you get one and don't be shy about using it if something goes wrong. Your board doesn't have to break in half to qualify for a warranty replacement—sometimes what looks like a simple crack or wrinkle can indicate a serious problem, like a delamination or broken core. If you notice something that bugs you, it's probably worth checking out.

Try the shop where you bought the board first to determine for sure if it needs repair or replacement. If they can't (or won't) help you, or if they suggest an expensive repair, try contacting the manufacturer as well. You'll probably have to pay for shipping and wait a week or two, but manufacturers are even more likely than a shop to stand behind the product. Just remember to hang on to your receipt and call ahead in case you need a "return authorization number." Then, any repairs or replacements covered by the warranty should be free. Even repairs not covered should be fairly inexpensive, especially if you put something nice in the package for the folks at the other end!

Test-driving

Some things you just can't tell by looking, and that goes double for snowboards. Certainly it pays to look carefully first and to narrow down the possibilities to a few clear alternatives before you start paying for demos. Then there's nothing like a test-drive to give you a feel for the differences between boards and to assure satisfaction with your investment.

The hardest part about testing boards is finding demo versions of the right models. Most shops have limited demo fleets, so you may have to ask at more than one place to find your top few choices. Friends are another likely source, or you could really strike it rich at a manufacturer's "on-snow demo." (As described under "Events" on page 134, these events bring large numbers of suppliers to resorts with all the latest gear available for a free trial.)

When dealing with a shop, be sure to ask about "demo" fees as opposed to rentals. Also, be prepared to negotiate. At the least, you should be able to apply the cost of a demo toward a purchase; a better deal would be to arrange to try several boards without racking up a huge tab. Start by explaining clearly that your objective is to try *at least a few* boards (not just renting one for the day), and let them know that you're serious about buying.

Once you've actually laid your hands on a hot new demo board, there are a few guidelines for making accurate comparisons. It's mostly common sense, but here's a quick laundry list.

- **Use the same boots and bindings for every board.** Otherwise, if something feels different, it will be hard to tell whether it's the board, the boots, or the bindings.

- **Use the same settings.** Stance width, stance angles, and various binding settings

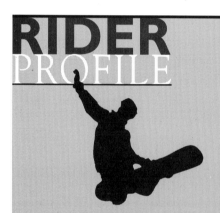

RIDER PROFILE

TARA GANUN
PR Queen with Fuse Sports
Marketing
Age: 28
Height: 5'3"
Weight: 128
Foot Size: 8½ or 9
Years Riding: 8

Tara promotes some of the biggest annual events in snowboarding, including the U. S. Open snowboard competition at Stratton, Vermont, and Boarding for Breast Cancer, an industry fundraiser for breast-cancer research founded in memory of early snowboard soul sister Monica Steward.

EQUIPMENT COMMENTS ◄ -
Tara rides a Burton Freedom 51, a freeriding board, with two-strap Burton Custom freestyle bindings and Burton Drifter boots, size 8. "My board is great on groomed but it's too short when there's powder. I'd like to try a 156. My boots are slightly stiffer than I would like but I can really drive them, which is fun. My old boots were too soft and hurt my feet when I cranked my bindings super tight. I haven't tried step-ins yet: The boots would have to be so dialed for me to really enjoy them, and I'm not sure they're there yet. I ride with my bindings completely cranked, and I don't think a step-in system would hold my heel down as well."

are all adjustable; use the same settings for each board so you know that whatever feels different is coming from the board.

- **Check the tune.** Snowboard edges are like kitchen knives—they can be razor sharp and slice through anything, or dull and useless for anything but butter. You can tell which is which by running your fingernail or skin *across* (not *along*) both edges. They should be sharp and free of chips or snags around the bindings but smooth and dull at the very ends. Ask for a board with sharp edges that have been de-tuned at the tip and tail, and you're good to go.

- **Go ride.** Testing snowboards is a lot like test-driving cars: You don't have to be a mechanic to notice how every board rides a little differently, or to determine what you do and don't like. All you have to do is pay attention—like "Wow, that was a snappy turn," or "Damn, that run felt awful"—and to put those observations together into an overall impression of the board.

- **Trust your first impression.** Don't feel you need to get used to a board before you can properly evaluate it. On the contrary, your first impressions are probably the most valuable. Take mental notes right from the start (unless, like me, you're actually anal enough to write them down) and above all, trust your instincts.

- **Go for variety.** To get more of a feel for a board's strengths and weaknesses, take it through a variety of terrain and maneuvers. For example, try both big, fat turns and tight little ones—some boards can handle both smoothly and comfortably, whereas others seem to get stuck in one type of turn. Also, try going both fast and slow—some boards can handle a range of speeds nicely; others tend to vibrate or chatter as you pick up speed. Finally, try a variety of snow conditions if possible—a few turns on some steep hardpack will tell you how well the board holds an edge, for example, while a few turns in some fresh snow will tell you how it floats in powder.

- **Switch boards often.** The ideal way to do a side-by-side comparison of various board models is to test them one after the other, preferably on the same day. That way, changes in temperature and snow conditions are less likely to affect your experiment, and your impressions stay fresh. It's a whole lot easier if the shop you're working with is right on the slopes, in which case it shouldn't be a big deal to switch boards throughout the day.

- **Try at least three different boards.** Any fewer and you're just not likely to get a feel for the alternatives. Any more can start to feel like work, even if it isn't pinching your pocketbook. Go with whatever works best for you, and don't forget to mix some fun in with all the concentration. You'll know soon enough when you've found the board that's a keeper.

"**S**oft boots are much more comfortable than hard boots, and you can utilize the entire mountain in them. You can freeride down any trail, hit the bumps, jump in the pipe and park, whatever you want to do. And, you can still carve like crazy down a groomed slope. Hard boots are so much stiffer that I find them limiting. I feel like I can't bend my knees and ankles in them, or get as low and drive through my turns, and it is more difficult to up-unweight. I just really prefer soft boots—they're more comfortable and the riding is much more dynamic."

—Greta Brumbach,
Research and Testing Manager, Ride Snowboards

BOOTS

Boots and bindings contribute to performance as much as any board. An old pair of Sorels and heavy-duty bindings may get you down the mountain, but they don't offer the same support, heel hold, and energy transfer as modern boots and bindings do. This is particularly true for women's boots and smaller bindings, which have been vastly improved in just the last few years. Consider your equipment as a three-part system (board, boots, and bindings), and it's important to get all three components contributing equally to your riding.

As with boards, the first step in choosing boots is to determine which overall category you're interested in: freestyle, freeride, or alpine (which requires hard boots). The biggest difference among the boots in each category is the overall level of support they provide.

Freestyle boots tend to offer the greatest overall flexibility for maximum range of motion in the pipe and park. Like wearing sneakers instead of a supportive hiking boot, this is accomplished with very soft shell and liner materials; relatively short cuff heights; soft and simple lacing systems; and flexible, shock-absorbing sole designs. The overall purpose is to keep you anchored comfortably to the board without compromising the freedom of movement it takes to tweak your legs (and board) into all those famous freestyle positions.

Freeriding boots also are "soft" (as opposed to being made from hard plastic shells), but they tend to offer much more support and responsiveness. Like switching up from sneakers to supportive hiking boots, this is accomplished with stiffer tongues, liners, outsoles, and shell materials; taller cuff heights with "power straps" that wrap around your shin; and sophisticated lacing systems that hug your feet for more support. These features provide slightly less mobility than a freestyle boot, but the payoff is much quicker edge response.

Finally, alpine or "hard" boots offer the maximum support, with stiff, plastic shells, super-supportive liners, and levered buckles instead of laces for a snap-tight fit. Not all hard boots are alike: Some feature shorter cuffs, relatively soft plastic shells, and only three buckles for a relatively large amount of flexibility in a hard boot. Others are taller and stiffer, with four buckles instead of three for instant carving response. You can't roll your ankle sideways as well and tweak into various tricks in them, but you can tilt your whole board sideways into those fast, clean carves.

BOOT TERMINOLOGY

Liner:

Liner quality affects comfort, level of support, weight, and durability. Good liners cup your foot in cushy support all the way around, hold your heel down securely, won't break down or pack out excessively, and are super lightweight. Cheap liners are dense, heavy, and don't fit your foot snugly. Freestyle liners tend to feature a laceless "overlap" design for freedom of movement, easy in-and-out, and no possibility of tongue float. (Some are "linerless," with a single layer of thick foam instead of a separate liner that pulls out.) Freeriding liners tend to lace up for a super-snug fit. Many new liners can also be heated and custom shaped to your foot, but watch out for big jumps in bulk, weight and/or expense.

Outsole and midsole

(soft boots only): Quality sole designs are lightweight, shock absorbing, stiff enough for traction and responsiveness, and yet soft enough for positive board feel. Materials such as compression-molded EVA decrease weight, while boots that are half rubber will be noticeably heavier.

Cuff:

Cuff height, shape, and material affect both support and comfort. Good cuffs wrap snugly around your lower leg, providing the desired level of heelside support without pinching or pressuring the bottom of your calf muscle. Bummer cuffs are too tall, stiff, and/or sharp, causing them to pinch or pressure the base of your calf.

Tongue: Tongue shape and material affect comfort, retention to the board, and, above all, toeside response. A good tongue is supportive, cushy, and carefully sculpted to conform or wrap snugly to the shape of your foot. Scary tongues are bulky or pinch on the sides, put pressure on the bones at the top of your instep, and flop or fold over at the ankle when you lean on them for support.

Shell:

Quality shells provide the desired level of support in a lightweight, waterproof package. Nylon and leather are common choices for soft boots. Nylon is more flexible, lightweight, and stretch-resistant, but it's not as waterproof or durable as leather. Leather is more supportive, durable, and waterproof, but it is also heavier and stretches more than nylon.

"**W**ith hard boots you can go fast, be precise, and carve. You've got much more control. If you want to relax, go with soft boots. If you really want to ride and challenge yourself, go with hard boots. It's much more exciting."

—Christine Rauter, world-class European alpine competitor and (obviously) hard-boot fan

A QUICK REFERENCE GUIDE TO BOOT FEATURES

Freestyle

(maximum flexibility for range of motion in the pipe and park)

- Low-to-moderate cuff height
- "Softest" shell and liner materials
- Lace closure with *overlap* (non-lacing) liner or one-piece, *linerless* design
- $125 to $250 (step-ins are usually more expensive than conventional)

Manufacturers
Airwalk
Burton
K2
Morrow
Northwave
Ride
Sims
Vans

Freeride

(moderate support for a blend of flexibility and responsiveness)

- Moderate-to-tall cuff height
- "Soft" but supportive shell and liner
- Lace closure with ankle and/or shin straps and plastic or otherwise reinforced tongues
- Removable, lace-up or thermofit liners
- $125 to $250 (step-ins are more expensive)

Manufacturers
Airwalk
Burton
K2
Knu
Nitro
Research Dynamics
Ride
Rossignol
Solomon
Vans

Alpine

(maximum support for instant carving response)

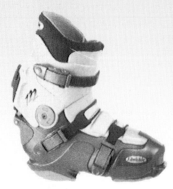

- Moderate-to-very-tall cuff height
- "Hard" plastic shell and super-supportive liner
- 3 to 4 metal or plastic buckles for closure (as opposed to laces), with removable overlap or laceable liner
- $300 to $450

Manufacturers
Blax (Generics)
Burton
Raichle

Of course, it makes the most sense to choose boards, boots, and bindings from the same style category, since they're designed to work together. However, it's not uncommon to match equipment from two of the three categories, like mixing a freestyle board with freeriding boots for extra ankle support.

Choosing snowboard-specific boots

We discussed the importance of snowboard-specific boots in Chapter 2, but here's a quick review. Regular winter boots can look similar to snowboard boots at a glance, but snowboard boots have all kinds of special features designed just for riding: supportive tongues and spines for power transmission where you need it; special lacing and buckle systems to protect your ankles and keep your feet sucked flat against the board; special soles for shock absorption and leverage over the edge; and sophisticated, lightweight padding to make all that support feel like your favorite old sneakers. Street boots more than pale in comparison—they won't keep you as warm or comfortable, and they won't begin to help you ride as well.

Sizing and fit

I can't overemphasize the importance of finding a boot that's a perfect fit. Here's what happens when you ride in a boot that isn't: The boot doesn't provide support where you need it, so your feet float around every time you go to make a move. Your toes search desperately for something to cling to; your arches ache from straining for something to push against; and your calves are wiped after about two runs because of all the extra work it takes to stay in control. (Did I mention they're also a great way to wind up falling on your butt a lot?) So, fit is king—or shall we say, "queen."

Conversely, here's what happens in a boot that really fits: The boot cups your foot in all the right places, so it responds instantly to every movement of your foot and lower leg. It is also supportive enough to keep your feet sucked down against the board, and to transfer every ounce of pressure straight to your edges. There is comfort but no play in the system, so gratification is instant—your board steers exactly in the desired direction, lifting effortlessly onto its edge in both heel- and toeside turns. Get great boots and suddenly you have the balance and control to ride with style all day long, and you're not even pooped. Aha! Or rather, aaaaahhhhhhhhh.

So, how do you find the perfect fit? Choose a women-specific boot, and get the right size.

Choosing women's-specific boots

Unlike boards, there seems to be universal consensus on this subject in the snowboarding community. It just seems to be a given that, as with other body parts, men and women have completely different feet: Men tend to have larger ankles, wider heels, a lower instep, a proportionately narrower forefoot, and higher calves; women tend to have smaller ankles, narrower heels, a higher instep, a proportionately wider forefoot, and lower calf muscles. As a result, the better manufacturers have developed completely separate men's and women's foot molds, called "lasts," for their men's and women's boots.

That said, note that not all so-called "women's" boots are built around women's lasts. These take considerable time and expense to build, so some manufacturers opt not to bother. A common shortcut uses men's lasts for the outer shell, with an extra 5 mm of foam in places to make the inside feel like it fits a woman's foot. The extra padding feels great in the shop but "packs out" within weeks, effectively returning the boot to a men's model.

To avoid wasting your money, be sure to specify not just a women's size, but a boot that was built inside and out around a last of a woman's foot. Also, be wary of excess padding. A "fake" women's boot is easy to spot, especially if you compare it to the same model in a men's size (that is, compare a women's 7 to a men's 5). On the outside, compare the ankle volume, sole width, and cuff height. On the inside, check the heel pocket, arch support, toe box, and calf flare. Real men's and women's boots will show obvious structural differences. Meanwhile, a men's boot in drag will look like just that: same as the men's model, but with a lot of extra padding and a dolled-up paint job.

Get the right size

So, we're down to *women-specific snowboard boots*, which are generally sized like street shoes. If you wear a women's size 7 shoe, you'll probably wear a women's size 7 snowboarding boot. The major exceptions are hard boots, which tend to be made in Europe and are sized in centimeters. Any shop should be able to do the conversion for you, or, better yet, let them measure your feet from scratch on one of those nifty sliding devices.

As for the fit of individual makes and models of boots, keep in mind that feet are as different as faces, and certain brands of boots tend to fit certain types of feet better. Also remember that human feet have a tendency to swell during the day. Plan to try on a bunch of different boots, be aware that your feet are smaller first thing in the morning, and wear the same socks you would use for riding (or slightly thinner ones, since all boots will pack out a little bit).

Of course, the true test of any boot is to try those puppies on. Your first impression is important—you can tell a lot about fit just by standing still. But it's also critical to spend a few minutes walking and jumping around. A well-fitting boot should hug your foot all the way around as it moves, from ankle to instep to toe box to calf flare. It should also keep your feet pulled firmly against the sole and shouldn't let your heels lift up. Do the "tiptoe test" (see page 28) to be sure, with the boots laced or buckled so they're nice and snug at the ankle.

(For the sake of comparison, a boot made from a man's last will often feel wide in the heel, loose in the ankle area, and possibly too snug in the toe box. Even those men's-boots-in-drag don't feel the same as the real thing. I tend to think of them as a little like Wonder Bras: All that extra padding can make a nice first impression, but it starts to feel awkward and bulky once you start moving around. For snowboarding, you're way better off with the kind of support that follows your every move—like a clingy but comfortable sports bra.)

Price points

Like boards, boots are made for a variety of budgets. High-end models use the most sophisticated features and materials to deliver ultimate performance. Traditional soft boots cost in the neighborhood of $150 to $250; hard boots cost about $100 more. "Price point" models tend to sacrifice some of the deluxe features and deliver bare-bones performance at a savings of $50 to $100.

My advice is to buy the best boot you can afford. Truly great boots offer carefully distributed response and comfort in packages that are lightweight *and* will keep your toes toasty warm. Cheaper boots may save you money, but the tradeoffs can include wet or frozen toes, foot pain, and just plain working too hard for your turns. Weight especially makes a huge difference on the hill: A few extra pounds may not seem important in the shop, but consider how much time you'll spend riding the lift, hiking the pipe, and/or just walking from car to lift. Heavy boots are literally a drag in each situation, whereas light ones tend to feel like flyweight running shoes in comparison. The extra $50 they cost may seem unnecessary in the shop, but it's not much of a savings when you're forced to head for the base lodge while your buddies make the most of their lift tickets.

- **Shell**: Quality shells provide the desired level of support in a lightweight, water-proof package. Nylon and leather are common choices for soft boots. Nylon is more flexible, lightweight, and stretch-resistant, but it's not as waterproof or durable as leather. Leather is more supportive, durable, and waterproof, but it is also heavier and stretches more than nylon. As for hard boots, plastic quality affects durability and the extent to which a boot's stiffness will change with temperature. Beware of boots that are soft and mushy in the shop, but keep in mind that even good plastic will probably stiffen up a bit out on the hill.

- **Tongue**: Tongue shape and material affect comfort, retention to the board, and above all, toeside response. A good tongue is supportive, cushy, and carefully sculpted to conform or wrap snugly to the shape of your foot. Scary tongues are bulky or pinch on the sides, put pressure on the bones at the top of your instep, and flop sideways or fold over at the ankle when you lean on them for support.

- **Cuff**: Cuff height, shape, and material affect both support and comfort. Good cuffs wrap snugly around your lower leg, providing the desired level of heelside support without pinching or pressuring the bottom of your calf muscle. Bummer cuffs are too tall, stiff, and/or sharp, causing them to pinch or pressure the base of your calf.

- **Liner**: Liner quality affects comfort, level of support, weight, and durability. Good liners cup your foot in cushy support all the way around, hold your heel down securely, won't break down or pack out excessively, and are super lightweight. Cheap liners are dense, heavy, and don't fit your foot snugly. Freestyle liners tend to feature a laceless "overlap" design for freedom of movement, easy in-and-out, and no possibility of tongue float. (Some are "linerless," with a single layer of thick foam instead of a separate liner that pulls out.) Freeriding liners tend to lace up for a super-snug fit. Many new liners can also be heated and custom shaped to your foot, but watch out for big jumps in bulk, weight and/or expense.

- **Outsole and midsole** (soft boots only): Quality sole designs are lightweight, shock absorbing, stiff enough for traction and responsiveness, and yet soft enough for positive board feel. Materials such as compression-molded EVA decrease weight, while boots that are half rubber will be noticeably heavier.

- **Step-in versus conventional boots** (soft boots only): Step-in boot-and-binding systems hold your feet to the board with an automatic trigger mechanism that usually grips your boot *from below*. These are widely known for their convenience, but they can also compromise heel hold, board feel, and freestyle mobility. Look for systems with the highback on the binding (as opposed to built into the boot) for increased comfort, mobility, and adjustability. Conventional boot-and-binding systems tend to use straps that buckle manually *over* your feet to hold your board on. While not as convenient as step-ins, these offer tried-but-true heel hold, board feel, freestyle mobility, and value.

- **Forward lean and flex adjustments** (hard boots and step-in boots with the highbacks either inside the boot or built-in on the back): Good hard boots have adjustable flex and forward lean mechanisms that allow you to customize the fit and feel of your boots. These adjustments are discussed in detail later in this chapter and in Chapter 6.

BINDINGS

More than just being the glue that holds your feet to your board, bindings affect performance as much as any boots do. As you flex and roll your feet around to fine-tune the pressure to your edges, good bindings provide carefully distributed support and freedom of movement according to your riding style.

Binding styles

As you might imagine, *freestyle bindings* are designed for maximum mobility in the pipe and park. Conventional models use straps; generally, there are two straps on each binding—one for your ankles and one for your toes. These straps are almost universally made of plastic, with plenty of cushy padding to keep your feet comfortable.

Beneath the straps is a binding *baseplate* that both cups your boot and anchors the binding to your board. Most baseplates are plastic, which is light, inexpensive, supportive, and yet flexible enough to bend along with your feet and board. Many other conventional strap-binding baseplates are made of aluminum, which is also light, strong, and relatively inexpensive. Strap bindings with aluminum baseplates cost about the same as plastic bindings, but they tend to be significantly stiffer.

The third major part of a freestyle binding is called the *highback*—a tall piece of plastic mounted on the back of the binding. This goes against the back of your boot when your foot is in the binding and gives you a platform to lean against in heelside turns.

STRAP-IN BINDING SYSTEM

• Two or three plastic straps with quick-release ratchet buckles fasten foot to board from *above*.

• Plastic or aluminum base-plates do not fasten directly to sole of boot

• Are not meant to be inter-changeable with step-in boots.

• High-end models have adjustable forward lean and rotatable highbacks for increased comfort and support.

• Tend to be cheaper than step-in bindings

• Manufacturers: Airwalk, Burton, Duotone, K2, Morrow, Ride, Sims, Solomon

highback

baseplate

two-strap freestyle binding offers maximum mobility

three-strap freeride binding offers increased support

baseplate

While a conventional freestyle binding's ankle and toe straps hold your feet firmly to the board, everything above your ankle is free to move around. This makes it possible to move your body independently of the board, bending or tweaking your legs and board into all those freestyle maneuvers.

Freestyle bindings are also available in step-in systems. Often compared to clipless bike shoes and pedals, step-in boot-and-binding systems replace the straps used in conventional bindings with mechanized baseplates and special parts built into the soles of your boots, so the system engages automatically as you step on it. The big advantage of this is convenience, since you don't have to sit down or bend over and buckle straps. However, step-ins lock your boot down from *below*, which can compromise heel hold and freestyle mobility. They also tend to require stiff metal and plastic parts to be built into the sole of your boot, which can affect board feel. Finally, some step-in systems also take the highback off the binding and build it into (or onto) the back of your boot, which can also limit mobility. For true freestyle performance, be sure to find a system with lateral sole flexibility, secure heel hold, and a highback on the binding.

As with boots, *freeride bindings* can look a lot like freestyle bindings at first glance. The distinction is that freeride bindings provide more support than freestyle models do. Features like a third strap that wraps around your shin, stiffer highback and baseplate materials, and side-entry (step-in) systems all make the bindings *less flexible* and *more responsive*. The result is a balance of freestyle mobility and carving response: As you flex and roll your feet around to make adjustments, the extra support or resistance from your bindings transmits this pressure to your edges. You may lose some ability to tweak in the park or pipe, but you also gain some ability to tilt your board into quick, clean turns. Supportive plastic tongues, "power ramps" under your toes, and highback wings that wrap around your calf are other popular ways to increase board control.

The purpose of *alpine* or *plate bindings* is to maximize response. Designed to go with hard boots, they use strong wire bails to clamp your boots firmly to the board. The result is very little play between you and your board so that every little movement of your feet and knees is transmitted directly to your edges. You can't roll your foot sideways in the binding for freestyle-like mobility, but you can tilt the whole board over into full-on, precision carves.

Like freestyle and freeride bindings, plate bindings are available in both manual and step-in models. Manual bindings tend to be more flexible and keep your foot closer to the board, but they require sitting down or bending over to buckle in; step-ins offer the convenience of snapping shut as soon as you place your foot in the binding, but they also tend to put extra parts under the sole of your boot. This can increase stiffness, response, and leverage, but may compromise board feel and forgiveness.

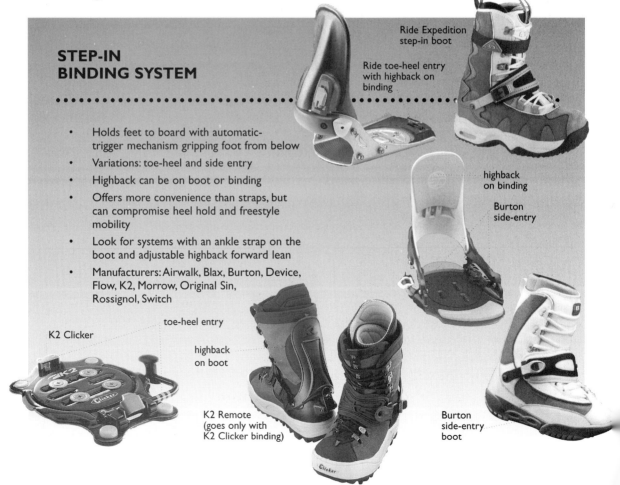

STEP-IN BINDING SYSTEM

- Holds feet to board with automatic-trigger mechanism gripping foot from below
- Variations: toe-heel and side entry
- Highback can be on boot or binding
- Offers more convenience than straps, but can compromise heel hold and freestyle mobility
- Look for systems with an ankle strap on the boot and adjustable highback forward lean
- Manufacturers: Airwalk, Blax, Burton, Device, Flow, K2, Morrow, Original Sin, Rossignol, Switch

Ride Expedition step-in boot

Ride toe-heel entry with highback on binding

highback on binding

Burton side-entry

K2 Clicker

toe-heel entry

highback on boot

K2 Remote (goes only with K2 Clicker binding)

Burton side-entry boot

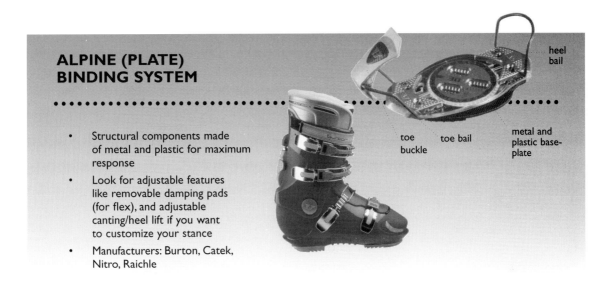

ALPINE (PLATE) BINDING SYSTEM

- Structural components made of metal and plastic for maximum response
- Look for adjustable features like removable damping pads (for flex), and adjustable canting/heel lift if you want to customize your stance
- Manufacturers: Burton, Catek, Nitro, Raichle

heel bail

toe buckle   toe bail

metal and plastic base-plate

Sizing and fit

Most bindings are available in small, medium, and large sizes, or they have sliding parts that allow an adjustable fit. Either way, the box or hangtag should list a range of corresponding boot sizes (for example, a unisex size small binding corresponds to U. S. women's size 5 to 8). Beyond reading the label, however, it's important to check a few key features. If the shop doesn't suggest a quick trial once your stuff is mounted, at least place your boot in the binding to see if they're compatible.

"**P**eople say that step-ins ride completely differently from straps, and I agree with that. In a step-in you're *pulling* with the bottom of your feet to get the board on edge, whereas in a strap binding you're *pushing* up against the straps. The energy transmission is completely different. Step-ins have come a long way in the past few years, but heel lift is definitely an issue. Then there's snow clog. You hear a lot about how step-ins are so convenient, but you don't hear about all the sitting down and picking snow out of the parts of your boot or binding. When it's just step and go they're great, but that's not always the case. Also, don't bother with the systems where the highback is built into the boot. The forward lean drives into your leg, which just causes major muscle cramps. Get a system with a regular boot, where the highback is built onto the binding. They're much more comfortable, and the forward lean is usually adjustable."

—Greta Brumbach,
Research and Testing Manager, Ride Snowboards

The general idea is simple: *Be sure the binding and boot fit together*. There are no "universal standards" for snowboard boots and bindings just yet, so certain brands of boots just won't fit in other brands of bindings. This is particularly true for step-in systems, where, for example, it's impossible to mix a side-entry binding with boots that clasp at the toe and heel. Conventional soft bindings and plates are easier to mix and match, but "square pegs" have been known to occur here, as well. You don't necessarily have to buy the same brand of boots and bindings, but at least be sure the components are designed to work together.

Once you've confirmed that your choices are fundamentally compatible, it's also a great idea to check the binding for fit. Like boots, baseplates come in different lengths and widths. A good sign is when the boot and binding fit like a hand and glove; a bad sign is when the baseplate is significantly longer or shorter than your boot. This means it could hang off the side of your board and trip you, or leave your toes dangling with nothing to push against.

Baseplates also come in "anatomically correct" versions, which is basically tech blah for distinct left and right shapes. These offer increased comfort and support due to the superior fit. (A nice secondary effect is that strap buckles and release levers, which can wind up in awkward spots on non-anatomical bindings, are positioned just where they're easiest to reach.)

Another key to well-fitting bindings is the highback. The fundamental purpose of a highback is to give you a platform to lean against in heelside turns, but almost no two are the same. Highbacks can be tall or short, stiff or soft, squared off or carefully contoured to match your boots. If nothing else, be sure the new trend toward "skybacks" doesn't leave you with a highback that's taller than the back of your boot (ouch). Better yet, be sure to get highbacks with lots of adjustments that allow for a custom fit. Like car seats, some highbacks can be tilted forward (for more support when your knees are bent) or tilted back and out of the way (for more freestyle mobility); some also can be rotated sideways for similar reasons, which is a particularly nice feature for typically low female calf muscles.

Price points

As with boots and boards, bindings are made for a variety of budgets. Some include all kinds of deluxe features and adjustments that offer optimum performance; others cut corners on features and materials, sacrificing performance in order to get you on the mountain with some cash left over for lunch.

Baseplates

- Conventional strap-binding baseplates are usually made of plastic or aluminum. Plastic is light, inexpensive, and flexible enough to bend or give with your feet and board. Aluminum is stiffer and more responsive.

- Step-in baseplates can be metal or plastic, and the binding may look "lower profile" than strap bindings. Just remember they look that way because half the parts are built into your boot. Most step-in bindings designed to go with soft boots are either side-entry or clasp at the toe and heel. Toe/heel systems retain more of a traditional soft-boot feel because your foot is free to roll sideways. Side-entry systems lock the sole of your boot down on both sides, providing less freestyle mobility and more lateral support.

- Carving or plate-binding baseplates are usually metal or plastic. Like hard boots, some use super-strong and stiff materials; others are designed to allow slightly more flexibility. Look for adjustable features like removable damping pads for flex, and adjustable canting/heel lift if you want to play with customizing your stance (see chapter 6).

Highback

- Consider height, forward-lean adjustability, rotation, and overall stiffness.

- Good highbacks are tall enough to provide the desired level of support without interfering with your calf muscle. Heads up on the new trend toward skybacks, which don't always fit comfortably with women's lower calf muscles. Also beware of "one-size-fits-all" models, which generally don't.

- Forward-lean adjustment devices (FLADs) should have a wide range of adjustment (women tend to prefer less forward lean than men do). Adjustability is key for adequate support. Look for "tool-free" designs that can be tilted back and forth by hand (as opposed to requiring a screwdriver for adjustments).

- Rotation and stiffness are also keys to comfort. Look for a sliding adjustment at the base of the highback indicating it can be swiveled sideways.

Straps (conventional, soft bindings only)

- Consider length, padding, and quick-release buckles ("ratchets").

- Look for straps that are specially contoured to the shape of your foot and cushy enough to be cranked tight all day and still be comfortable.

- Distinct sizing is important. Generic or one-size-fits-all straps pretty much don't.

Discs

- All bindings should have a friendly system for fastening to your board and for making quick adjustments to your stance angles and width.

- Look for a disc in the middle of the baseplate with legible angle readings on top and burly teeth on the bottom so you know your binding won't slide around.

CLOTHING

Unless you're headed for summer riding on the glaciers of Mt. Hood or British Columbia, the one sure bet about snowboarding weather is that it's going to be freezing outside. Thank goodness for all the studly new snowboard and outdoor clothing—which can keep the proverbial witch's mammaries cozy through a South Pole winter. It's no longer necessary to freeze our asses off in the name of winter recreation, nor even so much as shiver. Gear up, sister—the outside world is yours to enjoy in all but the ugliest weather.

Layering

We have already outlined the bare necessities of snowboard clothing: Three layers of synthetic fabrics, each built to allow moisture to evaporate from the *inside* without letting any in from the *outside*. Why? Consider the challenge facing your clothing: Its job is to keep your body cozy when it's freezing out, cool when you're roasting, and dry—whether you're sweating bullets or covered with melting snow. It's not so difficult first thing in the morning, when you're driving to the slopes or riding up the chairlift for your first run. But soon your heart rate and body temperature will begin to soar, leaving you sweaty by the time you reach the bottom—ripe for a bad chill on the ride back up. Over the course of the rest of the day any number of things can happen: Lifts stop, temperatures plummet, wind and clouds come out of nowhere.

"**S**ocks seem like such a little thing, but they're actually so important. People spend so much on outerwear and have learned that a good first later is worth the money. Then the perception is it's not worth spending $20 for good socks. But warm feet are worth it. The biggest thing is to keep your feet dry, so wicking is an important feature, plus synthetics tend to be fuzzier and more comfortable than itchy wool. Size is also key. It may sound like stating the obvious, but there's nothing worse than seams and wrinkles bunching up in your boots. Except cold feet!"

—Ali Napolitano

Sounds like a potentially hypothermic combination—and it is if you're caught in the wrong duds. But if you're sporting those nifty high-tech layers instead, it's hello warmth and comfort all day long. Your suit of armor is likely to be waterproof, wind-blocking, heat-venting, sweat-sucking, lightweight, comfy as bluejeans, and, of course, let's not forget *stunning*. A tall order just a few years back, but not today: Thankfully, high-performance snowboard apparel designed specifically for women is actually getting easy to find.

First layer

What defines a good first layer? First and foremost, it's the *fabric!* Warmth and moisture-wicking capacity are key, as well as an anti-microbial (read: stink-free) treatment and a soft "hand."

(What's the point of all that high performance gear if you're still going to opt for a cotton T-shirt?) Look for trademarks like Thermastat, Capilene, VersaTech, Coolmax, and other polypropylene or polyester-based materials. Weights range from very light to "expedition" heavy, and they come in everything from muted, match-all solids to wild and funky prints. They are largely inexpensive, and yet they're lifesavers.

As for cut, consider a top and bottom designed specifically for snowboarding. These are known to be roomy and non-restrictive compared to standard outdoor designs. Tops come in both long- and short-sleeve versions, with everything from boat- to crew- to "mock" turtle designs at the neck (snowboarders seem to find full turtlenecks too constricting). Pants tend to be standard, sort-of-tights design, not with feet but with cuffs and small side zips or slits at the ankle (in case you're allergic to bulk inside your boot). There are also "union suits" and bottoms with drop or snap seats, and even the occasional women-specific back-to-front access.

"**D**on't be afraid to buy your clothes a little big. Buy your first layer first and try outerwear over it. Then make sure you can do squats, bend over, and reach high and low before buying. Sure it's important to look good, but to me that's not the first priority. To me the worst thing is feeling constricted. Also, buy the best waterproofing you can afford, especially for pants. Vents are probably more important in a jacket. You're going to heat up and get cold later, and vents are so much easier than adding and peeling layers."

—Janet Freeman, designer and co-owner,
Betty Rides Clothing

For a snugger fit without sacrificing comfort, pay special attention to cuffs, seams, and the way the fabric stretches. Wrists especially are a key spot for comfort: Nice cuffs are snug enough to prevent snow entry and glove interference, but they're also loose enough for watches, bracelets, and blood flow. For pants, flat elastic waist bands bind less than drawstrings, and four-way stretch is way more comfortable than two-way. Also look for those special diamond-shaped crotches, which are tons more comfortable than four seams meeting up you-know-where. Don't forget that padded pants are also available if you're interested, and fans swear the extra bulk isn't noticeable.

Finally, why undo all that high-performance with soggy-diaper cotton underwear? The same warm, wicking fabrics used for long underwear are now widely available in women's briefs, sports bras, tank tops, and boxers. (I even know a few women who wear thick, cushy fleece bras, which they say are unbeatable for avoiding painful chafe.) And let's not forget socks, which are available in everything from flyweight to super-thick, padded versions. Just remember that multiple layers of bulky socks are a no-no, particularly if the purpose is to take up space in a boot that's too large. For optimum warmth and control, you're much better off with well-fitting boots and one pair of snowboard-specific thermal socks.

• •

"There's a lot of confusion about fleece and pile, which are different. Pile uses more acrylic and the knit process is different, so it's lighter, loftier, and has a higher warmth-to-weight ratio. You can wear less bulk and still be just as warm, which is nice if you're a woman and don't want to look like the Michelin man.

"The negative side of fleece is it doesn't block wind all by itself. That's why windstoppers and windblockers are doing so well. These pieces have the softness of fleece on the outside, with a laminated, windproof backing. [They are more expensive, but] you can choose less bulk and still get all the warmth of a thicker fleece."

—Sharon Leicham, Sierra Designs

• •

Thermal (insulating) layer

The purpose of the middle or insulating layer is to trap heat where you need it most. It also needs to take the moisture from your sweat-sucking first layer and wick it toward your outerwear, where it can evaporate. Luckily there's fleece, the softest/warmest/moisture-transporting/lightweight/easily-washable wonder fabric.

Not all fleece is equal, of course—it comes in countless weights and weaves. Thicker fleece prioritizes warmth; tighter fleece decreases wind penetration; and so-called "micro-denier" styles focus on skin-loving softness. "Pile" knits are lighter, less bulky, and offer superior warmth-to-weight ratios compared to traditional fleece. Again, the ultimate in lightweight, moisture-transporting performance comes with polyester fabrics, but common blends include acrylic, wool, and/or a small percentage of Lycra.

As for cut, this is one category where garments specifically for women have long been in plentiful supply. No matter what your taste, it's out there: jackets, vests, shirts, pullovers, zip-out liners, tights, shorts, leggings, sweats, pants, pants with ankle and side zips—even unitards! (I can't imagine trying to pee in one, but hey, whatever cranks your tractor.) Start with one, thick, storm-proof piece for ultimate coziness, or build a collection of lighter layers for a forecast-adjustable wardrobe. Chances are you've already got a closet filled with possibilities from other sports, but it's hard to go wrong with more fleece.

Outerwear

Ah, outerwear. It's the focal point of any snowboarding wardrobe and requires the biggest investment. No wonder we demand so much from it and all want style that suits us "to a T." Thankfully, this is another category where the choices for women are booming.

What defines great outerwear? Certainly *waterproofing*, or at least *water-resistance*, is critical. Given that all snow will eventually melt where it collects on your clothes, the difference in performance is in *how long* a garment will keep that water from seeping through to your skin.

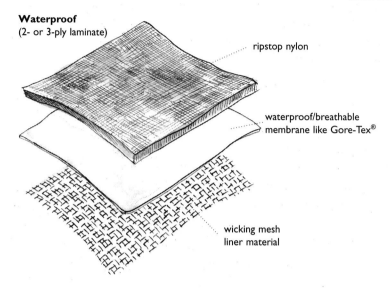

Waterproof
(2- or 3-ply laminate)

ripstop nylon

waterproof/breathable
membrane like Gore-Tex®

wicking mesh
liner material

MANUFACTURERS OF QUALITY WOMEN'S OUTERWEAR

• • • • • • • • • • • • •

Technical/ Gore-Tex®	Style Oriented
Wave Rave	Roxy
Morrow/	(Quicksilver)
Westbeach	Cold As Ice
Burton	Betty Rides
Convert	Sessions
(Columbia)	Deep
Patagonia	Sims
North Face	
Sierra Designs	

Truly waterproof pieces use special fabrics to be just that: capable of repelling water all day and longer, thanks to special micro-porous membranes laminated inside the fabric. Meanwhile, so-called water-resistant fabrics are made with less-expensive coatings (as opposed to laminated layers of micro-porous fabric) to shed water. These may keep you mostly dry most of the time, but sit or kneel in the snow long enough and water will seep through your clothes.

Of course, real waterproofing doesn't come cheap, so whether the investment is worth it for you depends on how much you want to ride and in what conditions. If you want to stay dry and comfortable for whole days at a time despite those unfortunate horizontal moments and/or powder dumped from the sky, you're going to need waterproof clothes. If you're only planning to head out for a couple of hours at a time, water-resistant fabrics should keep you dry until it's time to go home.

• •

"**A**nother option for super cold days is down. Down and synthetic down give you more warmth than fleece. They don't breathe as well, and real down isn't warm anymore if it gets wet. That's the big coup with synthetic down—it provides all the warmth of real down in cold weather but it also wicks and stays warm when wet."

—Ali Napolitano

• •

"At the bottom end in outerwear are $150 jackets. These have roll-on water-resistant coatings, which are not as waterproof as laminates. They do not have taped seams or a lot of performance features like venting and pit zips. At the other end of the spectrum are $500 pieces. These are three-ply, laminated pieces with a waterproof/breathable membrane, taped seams, durable water-repellent coating (DWR), and performance features like hoods and pit zips. They are the lightest weight, most breathable, most waterproof clothes. In between there's a big middle, with different grades of waterproofing and features. The difference is fabric, and the difference is features. That's where the costs come from, and that's what you pay for.

"Do yourself a favor and get women-specific clothing. Not that unisex or men's clothes are bad, but women's clothes are really different. The waist, hip, thigh, length, and other measurements are totally different, and they have real benefits. A lot of women are doubters—they think 'women's' just means it's going to look girly, or they're not aware of all the new, high-quality women's stuff. But there's enough variety now in women's clothing to suit all kinds of tastes, and the technical function is there. You may have to ask for it, but it's out there."

—Ali Napolitano

The second big buzzword in outerwear would have to be *breathability*. The assumption here is that, sooner or later, snowboarding is bound to make you sweat. Rather than let this moisture sit on your skin (and eventually freeze), good outerwear completes the process of helping it evaporate: First, your perspiration passes through those high-tech inner and middle layers; then the same micro-porous membrane that makes a garment waterproof allows your sweat to escape through your jacket and pants. Voilà! The cornerstone of all waterproof/breathable garments: high-tech membranes engineered at microscopic levels to let water vapor *out* (sweat molecules are really small) without letting any of the liquid kind *in* (melting snow or water). In less-expensive pieces (without the special membranes), breathability varies more according to the fabric insulation.

Which brings us to the dual concerns of adequate *warmth* and *venting*. The fact that both your body temperature and Mother Nature's can fluctuate drastically in a single day of riding emphasizes the need for highly versatile, or *temperature-adjustable* clothing. It starts at home with how much underwear and insulation you put on, and then depends on your outerwear. You can buy anything from thin "shell" pieces to highly insulated jackets and pants, sometimes with removable liners and/or mechanical vents. Most commonly in the form of pit zips (jackets) and side zips (pants), vents are like windows in your house or car: Open up for dumping heat when you're roasting and need some air, or shut 'em up tight to keep the weather out. What's right for you depends on how comfortable you want to be and how much you want to spend.

Okay, so far we've talked about waterproofing, water-resistance, breathability, warmth, and venting. What else helps make snowboard clothes terrific? The potential shopping list of features is endless, but here's a loose top-to-bottom sampler.

- **Pockets** in all the right places. You name it, it's out there: On the sides and lined with fleece for your hands; front-, center-, and top-loading for easy access from either side; up on your chest for goggle protection (with a liner that doubles as a lens cleaner); on the sleeve (with retractable key chain for your snowboard lock); inside for a Walkman; and see-through plastic for displaying your pass without having to unzip. There are pants with slash pockets in front for easy access even when you're sitting; cargo pockets on the thigh or ankle; and, of course, all kinds of butt pockets. There's outerwear with no pockets at all—sometimes to eliminate potential waterproof problems and sometimes just to save some dough.

- A removable or stowaway **hood** for sudden changes in the weather (or none at all if you're claustrophobic).

- **Fleece-lined** collars, cuffs and lower back panels on the pants for scratchless, skin-loving comfort even if your shirt comes untucked.

- **Reinforced zippers** with storm flaps for extra wind- and water protection;

- **Taped seams** that are folded over and double- or triple-stitched for durability, then backed with waterproof tape to keep water from leaking through the sewing holes.

- **Reinforced** elbows, butt, knee, and inside ankle patches to protect against scuffing.

- **Short jackets** for extra mobility, or **longer ones** for warmth and coverage (preferably with an adjustable, drawcord waist).

- **Adjustable wrist and ankle cuffs** to keep that sneaky snow out, especially in those unfortunate horizontal moments.

- Ditto for an **adjustable waist gaiter** or "powder skirt."

- **Glove and leash loops** for staying attached to your valuables, especially on the chairlift.

• •

"Get good gloves that really fit right. Women have smaller palms and shorter fingers than men, plus our hands get colder. That means we need super fit for warmth and comfort. Also, buckling your bindings is a pain if your gloves or mittens are too big."

—Ali Zacaroli, SnowSports Industries America

• •
• •

"Don't try to get away with sunglasses when it's gray out or snowing. They are fine if it happens to be warm and sunny, but people need to realize that the majority of the time you're going to need goggles. Look for the new women's goggles—some of them have smaller frames, which is an issue if you have a smaller face."

—Ali Napolitano

• •

ACCESSORIES

Just when you thought you were done, it's time for a few last items: hat, gloves, goggles, neck warmer, and a pocket tool.

Fleece is the way to go for itchless warmth on your head, and your hands will benefit from the best waterproof protection you can afford. Go with mittens for additional warmth. (Sharon Leicham of Sierra Designs recommends a windproof glove— "They are less bulky but still really warm!") A close-fitting thermal glove liner also is an option—then you can pull off your gloves or mittens to get at zippers and tissues without exposing your bare hands to the cold. Goggles or sunglasses are critical for protecting your eyes against the wind and sunburn (plus it's just plain hard to see with snowflakes flying in your eyes). Soft, cozy neck warmers are a "don't-leave-home-without-it" item for super-cold days, and they're more comfortable than a tight turtleneck or strangly scarf.

Then there's the pocket tool: An indispensable miniature screwdriver and wrench you'll need for the many little binding adjustments you will come to appreciate over time. Unlike the hefty versions for camping or home use, mini-tools for snowboarding are small, light, and incredibly convenient. The cool ones have special shapes and built-in ratchets for single-handed, no-hassle equipment tunes on the fly.

Last but not least comes lip stuff, sun block, water, a Powerbar, chocolate—whatever else you don't mind carrying to add a little something to your day. Beyond your basic three-layer system for overall warmth and dryness, it's pretty much whatever works for you.

Phew! I know all the choices can seem overwhelming, but don't let too much equipment research bite into your riding time. Start shopping in August or September, when all the new gear starts shipping to the stores. Visit a couple of specialty shops, grab a few catalogs, and read one of the fall magazine issues with a buyer's guide to all the latest gear. Then it's time to start loading up on the keepers and head for the hill as soon as snow flies.

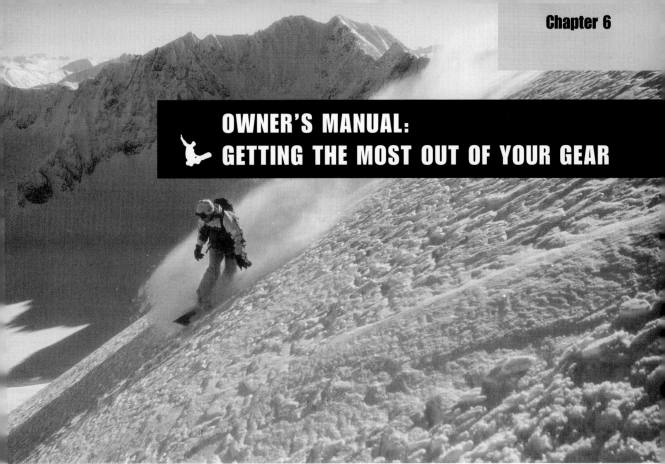

Chapter 6

OWNER'S MANUAL:
GETTING THE MOST OUT OF YOUR GEAR

Photo by Dan Hudson; Rider: Karleen Jeffery

Even if your new board comes from the shop with the bindings mounted, it's important to understand and experiment with your stance. It's just too easy to get set up inappropriately to begin with, and besides, everyone's "power stance" is a little bit different. Think of it like adjusting the seat and mirrors in a new car: Spend a few minutes getting situated and the rest of the ride is a lot more comfortable. Snowboard bindings aren't quite as easily adjustable, but they're close. Take your board out well before snow flies and it's a little like Christmas morning—a good chance to slobber/show off your new toy while you wait for the chance to actually use it.

POWER STANCES: MOUNTING YOUR BOARD

First, you'll need your board, bindings, boots, and just about any handy flat surface. (A floor with room to move around is nice, as is carpeting—it'll extend the life of your knees, edges, and floor.) Your bindings should have come with mounting hardware (screws), so the only tool you'll probably need to begin with is a #3 Phillips screwdriver. (Phillips means the "x" kind, not the "flathead" kind. The number 3 designates the size.) If you don't already have one, special pocket-sized versions specifically for snowboard bindings are available for about $15 to $30 at your friendly neighborhood snowboard shop. A potentially cheaper alternative is the basic hardware-store variety, which also makes a handy addition to any standard toolbox. A tape

A standard binding tool set: Pocket screwdriver, measuring tape, and pocket wrench.

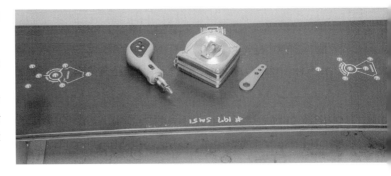

measure is also handy if you happen to have one around.

Once you've got the raw materials together, there are four main considerations that will affect binding placement.

1.   **Stance direction.** The first consideration is which way you'll face. Chances are you have already determined this, but the options are "regular" (left foot forward) or "goofy" (right foot forward). In case you're still not sure, it's usually the same way you would place your feet to slalom waterski, skateboard, surf, or run-and-slide on ice. (Not that you actually have to try this stuff—just imagining it usually is enough.) Another option is to stand up and have someone shove you from behind just hard enough to make you step forward with one foot: As long as you're caught unaware, the natural tendency will be to put the same foot forward as you would for riding.

2.   **Stance width.** Next comes the distance between your feet, known as your *stance width*. A rough guide is shoulder width apart, or about 18 to 22 inches for most women. If you're the lucky owner of a board with stance widths listed right on the deck, you won't need a tape measure to determine your stance width. Just stand on the board and get comfortable, feet about shoulder width apart, knees slightly bent, and use the markings to come up with a number (usually in inches). Another option is to relax, jump straight up in the air and land in whatever position comes naturally (horizontal doesn't count). The tendency is to land with your feet about shoulder width apart, so jump with a tape measure handy and then measure your feet from center to center. This stance width will be the same as the distance between your bindings. (Optional: Shoulder-width stance is pretty optimal for all-mountain riding, but many riders choose to put their feet wider apart or closer together. Wider increases fore/aft stability, which is handy for freestyle takeoffs and landings, but it also makes it more difficult to spin and to use your knees for carving. Conversely, narrower stances make it easier to use your knees for carving, and they actually make it easier to spin, but they also provide less fore/aft stability. Adjust the stance width by an inch or two according to your personal preference, or strike a balance for stability and spin. That's the beauty of snowboard bindings: Like furniture, you can always move them again later.)

3.   **Centered or back?** Now look at the top of your board, where the stance holes are conveniently spaced at 17, 18, 19, 20 (and so on) inches apart. The trick is to find the ones that match your personal stance width, taking into account where you want your feet to be with respect to the board as a whole. Like sliding a car seat back and forth, you can use different stance holes to position your feet forward, centered, or back relative to the center of the board.

Most people choose a stance that is either centered or back on the board. Centered stances are best for freestyle, since putting your weight smack in the middle of the board provides balanced performance for riding forward, backward, or spinning. On the other hand, shifting your stance back a centimeter or two gives you more forward-riding power for freeriding and carving. First, it helps turning performance (carving) by effectively softening the nose and stiffening the tail of your board, making for easier turn entries and snappy releases; second, shifting your weight back toward the tail helps the nose of your board float better in powder.

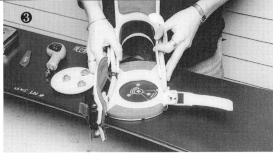

1. Find your stance width by measuring from center to center of each foot, which will also be the distance between your bindings (2). 3. Position binding over stance holes.

Look for information printed right on the board as a guide. At the least there should be an indication of the board's centerpoint, in which case you can bust out that tape measure to determine where to place your feet. (Keep in mind that stances are measured from center to center of each foot or binding.) It's not a bad idea to mark different stances for future reference.

4.   **Stance angles.** Finally, consider how far you want each binding turned toward the nose of the board. Recall that freestylers tend to like low angles (feet pointed straight across the board, as shown in the illustration on page 80), which makes it easier to ride switch. Alpine riders prefer lots of angle because their toes and body face down the mountain, which allows steering with the knees in both heel- and toeside turns. A moderate stance offers the best of both worlds for quality freeriding. A rough guide would be 0 to 15 degrees for freestyle, 15 to 30 degrees for freeriding, and 30 to 45 degrees for alpine.

Note that your back foot usually goes a few notches flatter than the front, so, for example, some typical stances would be 6 and 18 degrees (back/front) for freestyle, 12 and 24 degrees for freeriding, and 40

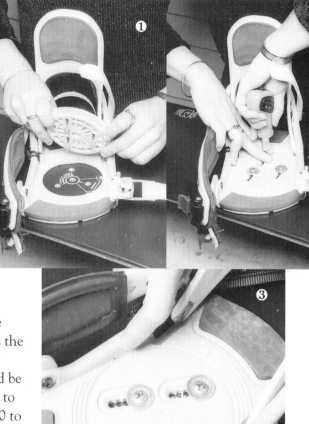

1. Inserting the binding disc. Note how the holes in the disc line up with holes in the board. **2.** Tightening screws. **3.** Rotate the binding to match the desired stance angle marked on the disc (barely visible in this photo).

and 45 for alpine. (These are just guidelines; individual preferences will vary.)

A range of angles should be marked clearly right on your bindings, most of which rotate back and forth around a disc in the center of the baseplate. Simply spin each binding around the disc until the arrows point to the angle you want. Then notice how the holes or slots in the discs conveniently match the pattern of the stance holes you picked on your board. All that remains is to line them up one over the other (a little like buttons and button holes). Then drop your mounting screws into place and start tightening them down with the screwdriver.

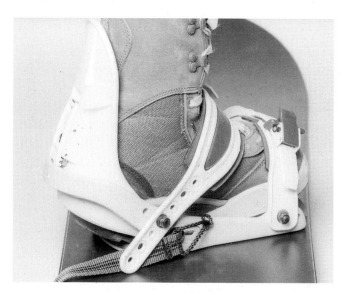

Checking for toe/heel alignment: For maximum balance and leverage, be sure the toes and heels of your boots are lined up directly over your edges.

Toe/Heel Centering

One last thing before you crank your screws down super tight: You may want to place your boots in your bindings to be sure the toes and heels line up over the edges. That is, you may need to choose either flatter or steeper stance angles based on the size of your feet relative to the width of your board. Double check this by placing your boots in the bindings and eyeballing their placement with respect to the edges. A little bit of room between your boots and the edges is okay, especially if you want to try a steeper stance for carving or a flatter stance for freestyle. Just remember that too much boot overhang can knock you off your edges, while too much distance between your feet and the edges decreases balance and leverage.

Also, be sure your feet aren't skewed off to one side or the other, which means your weight will be off center. If your boots are off to one side, try sliding your screws over in the little slots in your binding discs. This should enable you to move the binding toe- or heelward by at least a centimeter. Larger adjustments may require a different size binding. If your bindings are size adjustable, look for a way to slide the heelcup backward or forward and reposition your foot.

Crank those puppies down

Once your boots are lined up over your edges, be sure to crank down hard on the mounting screw. Loose bindings can lead to lost screws and worse—such as the freaky experience of having one foot pull out of your board. Start with them super tight for safety; then it's a good idea to check them a couple of times per season. (*Do not* use an adhesive compound, like LocTite, to try to keep the screws in tight. These compounds can break down board and binding materials. Invest in a pocket tool or keep your screwdriver handy instead.)

If you do happen to toss a screw, consider going to a snowboard shop (as opposed to a hardware store) for a replacement. It's important to get exactly the right length and thread, and the best way to do that is to use one from the original manufacturer. A screw that's too long can poke through the base of your board; one that's too short means you're only held in by a couple of threads. Also, the wrong thread pattern can ruin your board inserts. Bring your board and bindings (or at least one of the original screws) to the shop for a perfect match.

Adjusting straps

Conventional binding straps may also need to be fine-tuned to your feet. Most bindings have two straps each—one for your ankle and one for your toes. These are attached by nuts and bolts through holes marked XS to XL. Like your favorite belt, there's usually only one hole that fits just right. Consider that you want your straps loose enough to fit over your boots yet tight enough to clamp your feet down firmly. For the ankle strap, also note that the carefully molded instep padding usually has a "sweet spot" designed to sit over the "V" on top of your foot. Take a look, buckle in, tilt your board back and forth, and see how they feel. Even if your straps fit well at first, they may need to be moved down a size once your boots break in. (The strap bolts also tend to loosen up over the course of a season, so give them a crank periodically to prevent unexpected problems out on the mountain.)

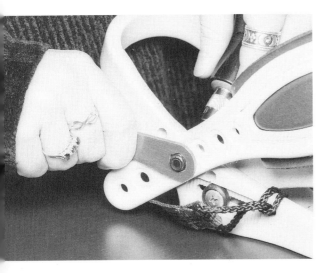

Sizing binding straps: Most have a range of size holes, like your favorite belt.

In addition to size adjustability, most ankle- and toe straps can be moved up or down on the binding. For example, toe straps often come assembled way down low at the end of your boots, though they actually are meant to sit over the ball of your foot. (Think about it: A strap over your toes means no circulation, and it doesn't really help you balance over your heelside edge. Meanwhile, a strap over the ball of your foot holds you like those old sandals from Dr. Scholl—secure but comfy, plus you can wiggle your toes.)

Look for an extra set of holes where your straps attach to the baseplate, particularly if you are out riding and experience any kind of foot pain. Simply moving them up or down a notch can alleviate pressure points and do wonders for your board control. As with mounting screws, just be sure your hardware is super tight by the time you're done. Trails of lost hardware and straps are all over the mountain, and the ride down is not much fun without them.

Forward-lean adjustment

Whether your highbacks are part of your bindings (strap-type and some step-ins) or attached to your boots (other step-ins), they probably came with some kind of *forward-lean adjustment*. Like the back of a car seat, highbacks tilt back and forth to provide just the right amount of support to your lower leg. Since your knees are bent when you ride, however, binding highbacks tilt *forward* (as opposed to reclining back like a car seat). Lots of lean means the highback engages as soon as you start rocking backward, tilting the board up on edge early and providing more support in heelside turns. Less lean means later response and less overall support, but more freestyle mobility because the highback is tilted back out of the way.

Adjusting forward lean: Loosening the center screw allows you to increase or decrease the forward tilt of the highback.

Specific lean angles will depend on the shape of your calves and boots, so your best bet is to try on a few different settings for a good fit. Look for a little gizmo that slides up and down on a track in the middle of your highback. (Sometimes these are tool-free, meaning you can unlock and slide them by flipping a lever like a light switch; other versions may require loosening with a screwdriver or hex wrench.) Simply slide the adjuster up or down to change the tilt angle of the highback, then lock or tighten down again.

Try both the minimum and maximum settings to get a quick feel for the difference (preferably with a wall or stationary object behind you to lean against). The big lean test is tilting your board up on its heelside edge, when you'll probably notice that too much lean digs into your calves. Meanwhile, too little lean makes it difficult to get the board up on its edge, so you wind up wobbling around and depending heavily on the wall for balance. Somewhere in between is a sweet spot that makes it easy to tilt your board on edge and yet won't force the highback to dig into your calves.

Finally, note that lean angles may not be the same for both legs. Again, it depends on the shape of your calves, your boots, bindings, and so on. Still, a successful combination for most of the women I've worked with is low-to-moderate lean for the front foot and a few notches more in the back.

Highback rotation

In addition to adjustable forward-lean settings, good bindings also come with *rotatable highbacks*. Like a chair that swivels, these can be moved sideways for better support and comfort. For example, say you want the extra support of higher forward lean angles, but tilting your highbacks forward causes the corner of one highback to dig into your calf. Instead of backing off the forward lean, try rotating the highback sideways to relieve the pressure point.

Not all bindings come with rotatable highbacks, so look for extra holes or a slot

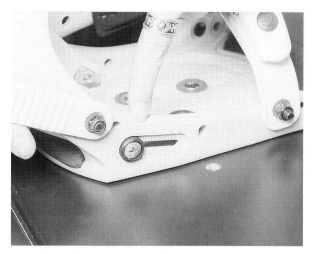

Highback rotation: Look for extra holes or a slot adjustment that enables you to swivel the highback for increased comfort and support.

adjustment where your highback attaches to the baseplate. Adjustable parts are usually designed to be loosened with a screwdriver or hex wrench, and then moved over by a hole or tooth-like notches in the slot. (Don't forget that moving one side of a highback usually necessitates moving the other). Even small adjustments can do wonders for comfort and control.

CUSTOMIZING YOUR BOOTS

Boot fit is so important in snowboarding that all kinds of special modifications have been developed to customize boots to individual feet. Two common options are *footbeds* and *boot liners* made of heat-moldable foam. These are designed to be popped into an oven and then cooled or set around the shape of your foot. More and more performance-level boots come with one or the other, but aftermarket options are also widely available for turbocharging whatever you have.

If you're interested in custom liners or footbeds, the first thing to do is ask at a couple of snowboard shops to determine what's most appropriate for your particular situation. Depending on how old your boots are and how well they fit already, you may want the help of an experienced snowboard bootfitter.

This professional help can cost as little as $5 for a butterfly pad to hold your heel down, more like $50 to $80 for custom footbeds, or closer to $150 for the whole shebang (custom liners and footbeds). If you have hard-to-fit feet, knock knees or bow legs, however, professionally administered orthotics or footbeds can add whole new dimensions to your riding.

Then there's the "do-it-yourself" option. Unlike bindings, boots don't always come with all the right parts to make them easily customizable to your feet. Unless a customizable liner or footbed came with your boots, you're probably looking at retrofitting with generic liners or footbeds off the shelf. These generally are cheaper than professional help, of course, and can still do wonders for fit. But they may require extensive trimming and/or padding to sit properly in your boots, and sometimes the ones that "pop in the oven" like to expand, shrink, burn your fingers, or do other unpredictable things. If you tend to be handy with these things, by all means go to it—just keep in mind that any "permanent" modifications to your gear (like cutting and cooking) are likely to void warranties. If anything less than total user-friendliness is more likely to annoy you, consider heading straight for the boot doctor instead.

One modification I don't suggest, even by a professional bootfitter, is adding a *heel lift* inside your boot. This rather disturbing practice started in the ski industry and has inexplicably gained recent popularity in snowboarding. Sold as an easy way for women to get their weight forward in skiing, the original purpose of heel lifts was to retrofit men's ski boots to women's feet. (Recall that ankle volume is much larger in a man's boot than in a woman's. Rather than build expensive new boot molds with smaller ankle volumes to hold women's feet down, heel lifts were a cheap and easy way to take up the extra space.) The result is a band-aid solution that, in my view, simply trades size problems for strength ones. Remember, one of the keys to strong snowboarding is a *stacked* skeletal alignment. This means standing in a position where your head, shoulders, hips, and ankles are lined up vertically. The alternative is stooping over and letting your bum poke out, which is exactly what happens wearing high heels: The lift knocks your knees forward and your derriere out the back, taking the load off your bones and forcing your muscles to compensate. Why compromise the natural strength and function of your spine? It all starts with your feet, which, as usual, are better off flat on the ground.

TUNING YOUR BOARD

Hair needs washing, teeth need brushing, and boards need a 10-minute tune now and then. Snow sliding alone will eventually dull your edges and suck all the wax out of your base. Rocks, stumps, parking lot abuse, and daily grinding against other boards in the car also can take a toll. Think of your edges as fingernails that develop snags, and of your base as needing an occasional coat of polish. Then all you need is the right file and some wax—or you can take the board to the shop for a full-on manicure.

Tuning at home

A quick edge file and wax job at home is simple, convenient, and, in many cases, provides a sweeter tune than shop jobs done by machine. You need a good file and a guide, or holder, which can cost up to $35 (but it will last several seasons). You also need some decent wax (about $5 to $7 for a season's supply), an iron (the $2 garage-sale variety is fine), and a few other low-dollar goodies to do the job at home. If you're a tech betty and into the hands-on approach, here's how it goes.

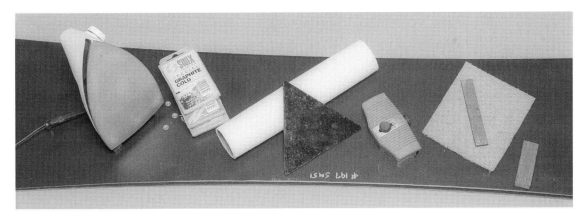

Typical tools for tuning at home: An iron, wax, paper towel, scraper, file guide, fibertex pad (same as a kitchen scrubby, without the soap), file (on the scrubby), and gummy stone.

Sharpen your edges

Sharpening your edges can seem intimidating until you realize it's about as difficult as shaving your legs. The hardest part is getting friendly with the sharpening file: Like a razor, snowboard files have little blades or teeth that sharpen and smooth the edge by shaving off the rough layer on top. Also like razors, files can be used freehand (about as easy as trying to shave by holding just the

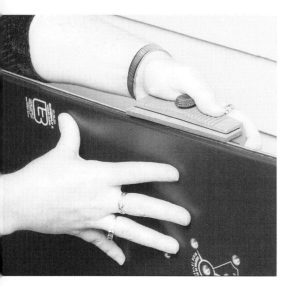

With a file guide, sharpening your edges is about as difficult as shaving your legs.

little razor cartridge) or slipped into user-friendly, hand-held *file guides*. These make sharpening edges as simple as a few long strokes with light pressure, pulling in the direction of the teeth, just as you would with a razor. It only takes a few passes on each edge, and there's not a lot of surface area to cover. The only real trick is to hold the file flat against the edge so it can't wobble back and forth and nick or round off the steel. That's what file guides are for: All you have to do is keep them pressed flat against the base of the board and the file automatically stays at just the right angle.

Give it a shot and it doesn't take long to figure out the particulars, like how it helps to hold the file guide as if it's a hand you're shaking, and to clean the filings out of the file regularly.

Another big help is to find a way to keep the board still while you sharpen it. Counter-top vices are ideal but expensive. A simple substitute is to kneel with the tail of the board between your legs, or to stand the nose on a chair and hold the tail between your knees. (If you do have a set of vices, face the base of the board away from you for increased comfort and leverage.) In any case, be sure to file in a garage or kitchen with sweepable floors, or put newspaper down to keep filings out of your carpet.

Wax your base

Snowboard bases are made of plastic that dries out over time, like a plant that needs water. The antidote is wax, which lubes the base and keeps it slippery for easy sliding on snow. Wax is available in different forms: Liquid wax comes in bottles or tubes and wipes on like furniture polish (but it also basically wipes right back off). A much longer-lasting alternative is solid wax, which comes in brick-like bars. You need an iron to apply it, but be sure to use an old one or buy a spare at a garage sale so you don't get wax all over your clothes. Actually, applying wax is as quick and easy as ironing a shirt or pants. All it takes is three steps.

1. **Prepare the base.** Lay your snowboard upside down on a couple of chairs or boxes, preferably in a garage or somewhere where it's okay to drop a little wax on the floor. Assuming you've just filed the edges, wipe the base clean of filings with paper towel and/or a clean

Cleaning the base with a fibertex pad.

fibertex pad (one of those little green kitchen scrubbies, but without water or soap). Liquid base cleaners are also available if your board is really caked with road grime, but both citrus and chemical solvent versions have a tendency to dry out your base. Meanwhile, brushing and waxing all by themselves will remove a fair amount of dirt, plus you don't have to use stinky solvents or wait for them to evaporate.

2. **Apply the wax.** Set the iron hot enough to melt the wax but not so hot that it burns and starts to smoke. Hold the iron pointy side down and press the bar against it, dripping wax back and forth across the board. This part is a little bit like pouring frosting on a cake: It's easy to go overboard, but all you really need is enough to spread into a thin film. Once you've dripped enough wax on the board, put the block away and use the iron to spread the "frosting" into a thin, even coat that covers the whole base. It should appear liquid and shiny. Don't stop the iron or let your board get too hot in any one spot. (You can monitor this by running your fingers along the opposite side, which should never feel hot to the touch.)

1. Dripping wax onto the board with a hot iron. Holding the iron upside down makes it easier to direct the wax into even ribbons. 2. Ironing the wax into the base. It's important not to let your board get too hot, which you can monitor periodically by feeling the other side with your fingers.

2. **Scrape and de-tune.** Once your edges are sharp and the board is waxed, let it sit and cool a while. Overnight is ideal to let the wax absorb fully, but the trip to the mountain is usually long enough if you wax first thing in the morning. Either way, lean the board against a wall or car bumper and give the base a once-over with a plastic scraper. This removes the excess wax that didn't absorb into the base—a little like scraping the gunk off your kitchen counter or a dirty pan. Hold the scraper at about a 45 degree angle (like a spatula or your fingernail) and you don't have to press very hard for the chunks to peel off in no time.

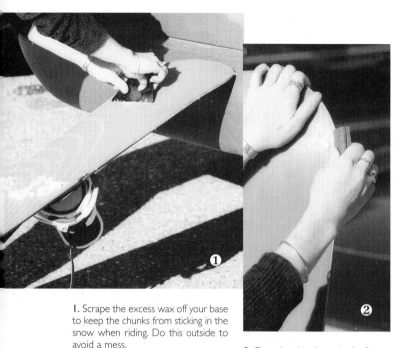

1. Scrape the excess wax off your base to keep the chunks from sticking in the snow when riding. Do this outside to avoid a mess.

2. Detuning the tip and tail of your board with a soft or "gummy" stone prevents edge catches.

Go lightly at first, and keep in mind that you only want to remove the thick patches and chunks, especially around the edges. Leaving a thin, even film on the base extends the life of your wax job. Finally, bust out a soft or "gummy" stone and "de-tune" your freshly sharpened edges at the tip and tail. Described by coach Paige Kunst of Women Only Snowboard Camps as "just like filing your fingernails," running a soft stone back and forth along the edge takes a bit of the sharpness off at the ends. This makes for smoother turn initiation and release, whereas the rest of your edges should be nice and sharp for optimum bite. Engineer Greta Brumbach of Ride Snowboards also suggests using sandpaper as an alternative to a stone.

Shop tunes

Shop tunes can cost anywhere from $15 to $45. A basic tune generally includes waxing and edge filing, both usually done by machine. Hand tunes may also be available by request, but they take longer and probably will cost more. Additional options, such as repairing a deep gouge in your base, can also cost extra.

Another popular service is *base grinding*, which smoothes both the base and edges by removing material from the bottom of the board. (Careful: You only get a millimeter or two of material to start with, and these are haircuts that don't grow back. To prolong the life of your board, avoid getting a base grind more than once per season.)

Call ahead to the shop for pricing and delivery information, and plan to leave your board there at least overnight. Also, consider that timing can affect your tune. Even a basic shop tune-up is better than edges full of chips and snags, but the day before a big holiday weekend is probably not the best time for primo-quality time and attention from a shop.

WATERPROOFING BOOTS AND CLOTHES

Over time, both clothes and boots can lose their ability to repel water. To prolong the effectiveness of special coatings and laminates, pay careful attention to the manufacturer's care instructions. In general, it helps to choose a non-detergent laundry soap like Nikwax Tech Wash for washing, which claims to "more than double the life of factory-applied water-repellancy treatments." Eventually, most fabrics will start to seep, however, at which point you can follow the washing with a waterproofing treatment. Nikwax's TX Direct washes in by hand or machine, and a new spray called Revivex is available from the makers of Gore-Tex. Check your favorite outdoor store for other options, but again, be sure to follow care instructions and read labels carefully.

"**A**lways follow the manufacturer's care instructions for clothing. A lot of the new high-performance fabrics should not be dry cleaned—it will break down the special coatings or laminates. If you have any questions, call them. That's what customer-service 800 numbers are for."

—Janet Freeman, Betty Rides Clothing

Boot treatments range from plain old beeswax to the same stuff that goes on your clothes. It depends on whether your boots are made from leather (in which case wax-based waterproofing treatments are an excellent choice) or a fabric like Cordura (in which case non-wax-based waterproofing treatments are better for maintaining breathability).

Keep in mind that many treatments will alter the appearance of your boots slightly (darkening the leather, for example) and/or may actually soften the material. Again, follow the manufacturer's care instructions for best results and read treatment labels carefully.

TRAVEL TIPS

There's nothing like a snowboarding road trip. Unfortunately, what's great food for the soul can completely trash your equipment. Whether you're going for three hours or three months, consider the following precautions for extending the life of your hard-earned gear.

Being small of stature has its advantages: You're cheaper to feed, easier to hide, and your board will probably fit in the trunk of your car.

• **Fold your binding highbacks down.** Not all highbacks will do this, but the safest way to transport bindings (other than removing them from your board) is to fold the highbacks down against the board and buckle any straps over them (conventional bindings only). This will decrease wear and tear, whether you put the board on or in your car, and will help guard against unpleasant surprises at airline baggage claims.

Padded board bags are a must for airline travel and preserving fresh car upholstery.

Car-top boxes are also an option to protect your toys from road grime, plus they'll fit a whole family of boards.

- **Get a padded board bag.** You can get 'em in just about any snowboard shop: soft and padded—but bombproof—duffel bags for your board. Basic versions have just enough room for one board with bindings attached; deluxe models come with locks, wheels, room for an extra board or two, and sometimes boot pockets for keeping the stink out of your clothes bag.

- **Put your board in the car**, not strapped naked to the roof. Ever catch doo-doo for being smaller than someone else? Well, now you have a comeback: You're cheaper to feed, easier to hide, and your snowboard is probably short enough to fit in most trunks. Say good-bye to road grime in your base and hello to better gas mileage. Put the base flat on the floor to save space, or lay multiple boards base-to-base on their sides. Just be sure to use a dry cloth or old towel if you're allergic to wear-and-tear from sharp metal edges. Wax is not a major concern unless you just put it on; put the board in sideways or upside down if you're worried.

- **Car-top boxes are also an option** for multiple copilots, or if you have a board bag that won't clip into a standard roof rack. Just be sure to wipe your board(s) down before they go back in the bag at the end of the day. Boards that are "ridden hard and put away wet" will rust around the edges. Back seats are not a good storage spot—melting snow and sharp edges can do unpleasant things to your upholstery, and boards have scary projectile potential in the event of an accident.

SUMMER STORAGE

It probably goes without saying, but clothes and boots should be put away dry in a puppy- and rodent-proof place. Boards should also be given a thick coat of wax or the base will grow dry and hairy over the summer months. I know it's short and sweet, but that's all there is to it.

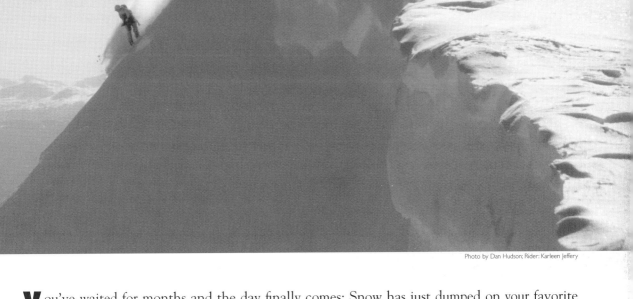

Chapter 7

A MAKE-YOUR-OWN MOUNTAIN ADVENTURE

Photo by Dan Hudson; Rider: Karleen Jeffery

You've waited for months and the day finally comes: Snow has just dumped on your favorite resort and your buddies call to discuss a snowboard trip. It's only _____ (5 minutes/5 hours/5 days) to the closest mountain, so you figure what the heck. It's going to be a whole _____(day/weekend/long weekend/week/season/lifetime) of adventure, and you are practically wetting your pants with anticipation.

A plan develops quickly: Whoever has the biggest SUV with four-wheel drive and CD player agrees to drive. Whoever is the best navigator/DJ rides shotgun, and your _____ (best friends/significant others/kids/coworkers/pets) are all going to cram in back. The weather service is forecasting another snowstorm, so you are leaving _____ (Thursday night/Friday afternoon/really early Saturday/next week/next Christmas/RIGHT NOW).

Time to assemble the requisite goodies, so you open your _____ (dresser/closet/gear closet/cupboards/garage/all of the above). You _____ (are/are not) going straight to the mountain, so you start by _____ (wearing/packing) your snowboard clothes. Let's see, the weather service says the temperature on the mountain is _____ (above freezing/below freezing/cold/really cold/yikes, below zero). You load up on _____ (light/heavy) socks, long underwear, and insulators accordingly. Then come your jacket and pants, and a _____ (baseball hat/warm fleece hat/super toasty hat and neck gaiter) because it's so dang _____ (warm/cold) out. Finally, in your handy _____ (day pack/duffel bag/embarrassingly large stack of suitcases) goes _____ (gloves/mittens, goggles/sunglasses) and those indispensable pocket items: _____ (choose any three: cash/sun block/Powerbar/lip goo/mini-tool/water pouch/walkie-talkies/herbal supplements/chocolate!).

    Phew, almost there. One last checklist before you get out the door: board, boots, bindings, street shoes. Even if you wear your snowboard boots for the drive to the mountain, there's nothing like a pair of _____ (Ugg boots/Birkenstocks/Tevas/Nikes) to slip on and soothe your feet at the end of the day. Oh ya, and the all-important cash card for _____ (coffee/lunch/lift tickets/the bar tab)—if there's anything you can't cover with the cash already in your pocket, you can always stop at the ATM. There's nary a base lodge without one these days.

    With a honk and a slam of doors, the fun begins. You load up the CD player, bust out some snacks, and formulate your plan for the first day. Someone _____ (called/logged on) to the snow report for the mountain, and the conditions are listed as _____ (powder/packed powder/frozen granular) with ____ (12/6/3/1/zero) inches of new snow. After much discussion, you make plans to spend the day riding _____ (powder/trees/carves/bumps/pipe/all of the above).

Jennie McDonald riding the stuff that snowboard dreams are made of: thigh-high powder. (Photo by Dan Hudson)

POWDER

Sure enough, a snowstorm has hit and deposited 6 to 12 inches of the lightest, fluffiest imaginable snow. It's a powder day! Thank goodness your buddies called early—you arrive at the mountain a full 15 minutes before the lifts open. You pull your boots and clothes on, grab your freeriding boards and lift passes, and head for the lift.

    The chair hasn't started running yet, so you have a little time to inspect the crew of regulars who have beat you there. These are the die-hard local powder junkies: Not the glamour crowd, but dedicated snowboard bums who pass up the benefits of 9-to-5 work and double- or triple-up on roommates, all for mornings like this. You notice they are all wearing hats pulled fast over their ears, goggles for eyewear, and jackets zipped up to their noses to keep the snow out. On their feet are noticeably long boards with large, high noses, which you now recognize as freeriding or "powder" boards.

    Just then the lift starts moving and the first row of ski- and snowboard patrollers jumps on (you can tell they're patrollers by the red jackets with signature white crosses on the back). Almost as noticeable as the jackets are the toothy grins they sport from ear to ear. Those bastards—no matter how early you come to the mountain on powder days they always get first chair. "Making sure the lift is safe," and all. Oh well, they earn it. So you pipe down and take your place on the chair, well behind the dawn patrol and maybe 15 chairs of locals. (This time!)

The snow gets deeper and deeper as you gain in elevation, and the mountain seems somehow asleep in the half-light of morning. There is not a soul to be found coming down the trails yet, and the whole mountain is noticeably quiet except for the hum of the chairlift. Even the storm has passed, so it isn't windy or snowing. Hm. In all the hype and hubbub you have heard about snowboarding, peace and stillness are not what you have come to expect.

A few minutes later you near the top, and the somewhat charged atmosphere of the race for first tracks resurfaces. The wind picks up as you clear the treeline and in the distance you can hear the whoops and yells of the happy souls who got there first. Before they even get off the chair your companions are buttoning the powder skirts in their jackets, and you can't help reaching down to tighten your front ankle strap. Since riding in deep snow requires a little extra pitch, you have already agreed on a moderately steep but wide open trail for your first run.

Practically jumping off the chairlift, you skate to the top of the designated trail and fasten your back bindings as quickly as possible. It's always like this on a powder day: A rush to get in as many runs as possible before all the fresh snow gets tracked out.

Finally, you're ready to shove off. Somebody picks the right side, someone else hugs the left, and whoever's left chooses side-by-side lines down the middle. It's hard to get moving in a customary stance, so you lean way back until most of your weight is on your rear foot. This brings the nose of your board up and out of the snow, so it's much easier to get going. Suddenly there you are—floating improbably down a sea of frozen, spraying ice crystals.

The sensation grabs the pleasure center of your brain and whips it into overdrive, only slightly limited by the fact that you haven't quite got it yet: How you have to keep your weight shifted back toward the tail, so the nose of your board will float and not submarine to a stop; how it helps to jump a little from turn to turn, so your board clears the snow and becomes much easier to steer; and how the whole process is refreshingly effortless once you find the sweet spot.

Eventually it dawns on you that you don't have to bother controlling your speed. Having powder up to your knees does that for you, so slowly but surely you make adjustments and discover what it's like to let your board run. Another realization—*you don't have to carve in powder.* In fact, you barely need your edges at all. Rather than tilting your board way on edge and driving the sides down into the snow, you need just a light touch with your feet. Yes, it's definitely more about playing the whole base against the thick blanket of snow, like spreading frosting with a knife instead of using it to cut.

Of course you toss it a couple of times, especially when you decide to launch off an upcoming four-foot drop. Ordinarily you would never have considered it, but powder does that—it makes you feel invincible. It hardly matters if you land right side up; all that snow is such a cushion that you barely feel it when you crash. So the next run you try the same drop again, and a few runs later you come back and land it. Once you even go for a 180, but it doesn't work at all—landing backwards is impossible in powder because the tail of the board submarines instantly. This tosses you into a cartwheel but it doesn't hurt, so who cares? It's just fun to try with all that snow to soften the landing.

By now the sun is overhead and each square foot of snow lights up with a thousand tiny sparkles. The muscles in your back leg are screaming from leaning back, you've probably got a pint of snow in your nostrils, and even opening every zipper in your clothing is hardly enough to cool you off. On the lift you undo the side zips of your pants, but then forget to close them up again and wind up with a front leg full of snow. It still doesn't matter: Your heart pounds more with delight than exertion, and the perma-grin on your face can only be described as shit-eating. No doubt about it: One morning of virgin "pow" runs, and you're a bona fide junkie.

TREES

Sooner or later the trails get tracked out, the snow grows moist and gluey from the sun, and masses

of people have arrived since your first few runs. Now would be a good time to stop for food and water, except there's a whole other mountain of powder waiting to be ridden in the woods. So you pant your way through one more lift line, grab a chair with your buddies, and trade and gobble the contents of your pockets. Someone brought granola bars, someone else brought water, and someone else brought an herbal concoction called ginseng chew. The buzz is better than a double mocha latte, and soon everyone is lubed, refueled, and ready for more fresh tracks. So much for lunch; it's time to head for the trees.

Trees. Just the word is enough to inspire a cautionary voice in your ear. You've heard the stories: Lost riders who eventually emerge on the wrong side of the mountain, sometimes after spending a frozen night in the woods. And the injuries—broken arms, boards, knees, heads. Sure enough, the risks are real—no one is there to think for you, to clear or mark hidden obstacles, to direct you around areas of danger or to point the way home if you get lost. Worse yet, no routine ski patrol sweep is going to come by and bail you out if you get hurt.

Hence the first rule of riding in the woods: The stakes out there are different, and you must be prepared to accept them. For some the challenge is part of the attraction, but for others it becomes a reason to sue the resort if something nasty happens. If you would even consider this—ever—then you must not go in.

Pro rider Leslee Olson carves a line between trees. (Photo by Patty Segovia)

Repeat: It is not the ski area's job (or mine) to babysit you in the woods. It's yours. If you're not prepared to accept sole responsibility for whatever happens, good or bad, then you must turn back.

But of course you don't have to go deep into the wilderness all at once. You can stick close to established trails first, riding in and out of the trees just to get a feel for it. Your resort of choice may even have "glades." These are open-forested areas where the trees are widely spaced, patrolled and maintained just like any open trail. Here you can get acquainted with the tight spaces, the fallen trees and branches, the streambeds and other unmarked obstacles that come with the territory. Hazards, yes, but manageable—

Don't try this at home: Michelle Barnes gets friendly with a tree.
(Photo by Patty Segovia)

and you get to make turn after turn in ridiculously deluxe powder. Better yet, there's often no one there to enjoy it except you and your buddies.

So you make use of the buddy system, and maybe even splurge together for a bunch of walkie-talkies (unless, of course, the whole point for you is to get away from modern communication devices). If you're not claustrophobic you also wear a helmet, because trees don't move as quickly as people if you get out of control, and they're a lot harder should you accidentally hit one.

Eventually you contemplate going deeper into the woods. You know the layout of the mountain—where to go in, where you'll come out, and what to expect in between—and someone who has been there before is with you to lead the way. So you go for it, and discover that poking around in all the chutes and gullies, often with no obvious signs of civilization other than you and your riding partner, offers a doubly potent fix of solitude and adrenaline. You ride, ride, and ride some more, and still can't get enough. Sometimes you get stuck in a flat spot and have to hike down; sometimes you hit unexpected steeps and have to hike back up. But the adventure is more than worth it, and leads you to collapse in happy exhaustion when you make it home in one piece.

CARVING

Rats. It's not a powder day at all but clear and sunny, with no new snow. All but the steepest trails on the mountain have been groomed into fields of smooth corduroy, and the conditions are ripe for carving. So you poke through your pockets and find a slip of paper from a party the other night: "Carving buddy, Christine, 555-7925." There are maybe 10 people who ride hard boots at your home mountain, and Christine is the only other girl. You were both so psyched to finally

Pro rider Betsy Shaw demonstrates a world-class carve.

meet an alpine compadre that, despite never having met before, you made tentative plans to ride together. Your other buddies are more interested in freestyle, so you make plans to meet up with them later and head for the designated time and place.

Sure enough, there's Christine, and the two of you head for the lift. On the way up you discover she's a part-time snowboard instructor. Out of habit, the first thing she does after you've said hellos is to check out your setup: three-buckle hard boots, plate bindings mounted at 39 degrees (back) and 45 degrees (front), and a board that's just the right width for your feet. It's not a race board (too stiff and unforgiving), but a high-end recreational carver: slightly flared nose and tail, slightly softer flex pattern (but still snappy enough to bounce back when you bend it), and slightly shorter length than most race boards (for easier turning). Great stuff on the whole, except the boots aren't made from a woman's last. Almost no hard boot shells are, so as the padding in the liners packs out you've started to notice some heel lift. This seems ridiculous given that they cost over $300, but Christine explains how plastic molds are really expensive, and manufacturers are betting you can't tell the difference. "Just add a heel lift under your foot," you've been told, but you already know that's a lousy fix. Christine recommends a custom liner instead—the kind that's injected with foam around your foot while you're actually standing in the boot, so it takes up the extra space *over* your foot instead of *under* it. They cost about $100 and they'll make your boots heavier, she says, but it's better than trying to ride in high heels.

Finally, you get to the top of the mountain and head for the flattest freshly groomed trail you can find. It's early yet so you have the place to yourself, which was part of the plan. Nice. Like learning how to drive in an uncrowded parking lot, you can now try carving turns without the threat of a collision.

Christine goes first, executing a string of flawless carves back and forth across the trail. You notice she's not moving that fast, and it strikes you how much she travels *across* the trail instead of down it. Sure enough, Christine explains, that's what carving is all about: The harder you bend your board into a turn, the more it carries you across the trail. You also have to dig the edge in so it *tracks* instead of sliding out. Start by putting your board on edge right at the top of the turn, says Christine, and then push against it so the board bends into a semicircle. She points out the hourglass shape of your board and talks about sidecut (sidecut? you ask), and she explains how each edge is curved, like part of a circle, so that it will make turns of the same curved shape. When you tilt the board on edge and bend it into a turn, it follows the shape of the sidecut. Yours is more pronounced than hers, which makes it easier to turn. Go ahead, says Christine, try it.

So you point your board down the trail, tilt it way up on edge, and push for all you're worth to bend it into a semi-circle. In response, the board picks up speed, holds an edge like you never would have thought possible, and then shoots off across the hill in a shockingly sideways trajectory. You let out a yelp of surprise and hang on for dear life. It's all you can do to keep up with the thing.

Wondering what the heck just happened, you are surprised to find Christine cheering as she waits below. "WAY TO GO! YEAH!" This can't be right, you think, but it probably is. Now all you have to do is to learn to keep up with the board.

So you do the same thing again, and again, and again. With each turn you focus first on pointing the board downhill, then on tilting it way up on edge and bending it deeply with your feet. Then you squeeze with your abs and can for the rodeo ride that ensues. Ten turns later you are somewhat used to it, and the rhythm of carving starts to make sense: Start the turn, bend the board, let it shoot you out again. At first it really takes you for a ride, but eventually you get used to it and even learn to control and direct it. You also start to remember the habits you learned from drills early on: head and shoulders stacked; hips tucked under; hands in front and level, as if on a tabletop.

Ten runs later you are still on the flattest groomed trail besides the bunny slope. Christine counsels patience—it is immeasurably easier to learn to carve on the flats first, and then move up to steeper terrain only after you can control your speed. Actually, it's starting to be so much fun you could care less if the trail you're on is designated green (easiest). You could also care less about the skiers and other snowboarders (yes, even other snowboarders) who give you static for riding hard boots. It's leftover anti-skiing mentality, or something like that, but who cares? The thrill of speed is just as brain-consuming as the thrill of air, and they have no idea what they're missing. By now you have stuck a few turns and soon forget all about them.

Eventually you figure out that carving comes in varying degrees: You can push with all your might through each turn, ricocheting back and forth from one edge of the trail to the other. Or you can back off and press lightly with your edges, letting the sidecut of your board do most of the work. Either way it's about playing your weight against the board: First you tilt it up on edge, then you throw your body weight against it so it bends. The board first absorbs all that energy and then shoots it back like a slingshot, conveniently launching you into the next turn. The harder you push on the first part, the harder it snaps back at the end. Christine demonstrates, first with easy, sidecut carves, then by working her board for all it's worth. It may take a while, but you'll get there, too.

Betsy Shaw carving the bumps at Sugarbush, Vermont.

BUMPS

It's not a powder, or even a packed-powder day, but one of those slushy spring days when the moguls get soft and forgiving. Bent on attacking that bump run you've been eyeing for ages, you talk your buddies into giving it a shot. All the way up on the lift you give each other a pep talk, and upon arrival you head straight for the top of the bump trail. Then one glance down the belly of the beast promptly deflates your confidence to oblivion. *Geez, I don't remember it looking that steep,* says that little voice. *Maybe we should take a warm-up run.*

Which is actually a great idea, so you do. Choosing a nicely groomed "cruiser" run, you do a couple of donuts to get your board underneath you and then ride down just hard enough to get a little winded. There. Your muscles are warm and primed, but you still have a whole day's energy to spend. Time to stop procrastinating and head back to the moguls.

Sure enough, it *does* look steeper than you remember, but all trails are that way—deceptively steep from above, somehow much less so from the bottom. This doesn't do much to bolster your confidence, but it's a fact. Okay, one step at a time.

You work on "picking a line." It's the first big secret of riding bumps: Finding a place where the moguls stack up in an orderly, zigzag pattern, so it's easier to get a consistent rhythm going as you make turns between them. In comparison, messy bumps jumbled one on top of the other are next to impossible to ride.

So you cruise back and forth across the top of the trail, peering down the field of moguls and mentally drawing lines between them. The lines go not on top of the bumps but down in the troughs between them, like where a stream of water would flow. This is the fall line, where gravity will also naturally feed you and your board.

At first all you see are those messy jumbles

Note how Betsy's line is evident between the four bumps in this photo, which line-up in an orderly, zig-zag pattern.

of bumps, but eventually a line sticks out where three or four troughs connect. The zigzag they form is actually rounded off, like the bumps themselves, and so after a moment's reflection they start to resemble a string of turns. Aha! Right, there's your line.

The next big challenge is going to be controlling your speed. Recalling hockey stops from early on, you make one quick turn around the first bump and then come to a complete stop just above the next one. It works, so you do the same thing again: Heelside turn around one bump; stop above the next one. Toeside turn around the next bump; stop when you reach the other side. You must be able to do this smoothly before you can link turns comfortably.

By now you will have wobbled, tipped over, or at least sat on a bump a few times (they can be handy that way). Sure enough, it's harder to balance when the ground is bumpy. So again you remember the keys to good balance—get firm, get low, get centered. And because the ground is uneven, *absorb*: Like riding a bike through an obstacle course of speed bumps and potholes, you have to alternately pull your board up and punch it down a little to meet the ground. Take it slow and look ahead by a few turns, and your body will know what to do by the time you get there.

Toward the bottom, the bumps flatten out. Each mogul is smaller than the last, and there is more distance between them. Here is the spot to start linking turns. So you traverse the hill, again looking at the various lines, and choose one. Below is a smooth and flat runout, so you really let it run on the last few bumps. By now you have a feel for the rhythm and your legs pump the contours of each. High fives go all around for the heroic finish, and you've still got plenty of time for another attempt before lunch.

So you go back for another run or two, but that's it. You don't want to kill yourself—bumps are exhausting at first and muscles can't learn when they're pooped. Two or three runs can take almost as many hours, and then it's time for a well-deserved rest.

RIDING PIPE

It's warm and sunny all right, and the resort has just finished shaping a new halfpipe. You and your buddies grab your freestyle boards, stuff a pack with water and snacks, and plan to spend the day there. Realizing that a first day in the pipe can involve as many tumbles as a first day of snowboarding, you have brought knee pads, wrist guards, butt padding, and a helmet. It feels a little like dressing for "American Gladiators," but what the heck. A day of looking potentially clunky beats a night on the couch with ice on your tailbone. You can shed the protective gear once you get more comfortable.

Pro rider Victoria Jealouse was a downhill racer on the Canadian national ski team until she discovered snowboarding. Back then her nickname was "crash." Now she makes the big bucks riding every day, has her very own signature model board from Burton, and her best friend Judy gets paid to draw her graphics. (Boys' club? What's a boys' club?) (Photo by Patty Segovia)

Olympic silver medalist Stine Brun Kjeldas wows the crowd at the U.S. Open.

Sure enough, the pipe is a beauty: Each wall has huge but perfectly smooth semi-circular *transitions* topped by a small section of *vert*, or vertical wall. The snow is not too firm, but not so mushy that it's super slow. They even put in a sound system so you can plug in your favorite CD. This is gonna be great.

So you pull out your mini-driver and stare at your stance. Let's see: Super-low stance angles? Check. The closer to zero your angles are, the easier it is to ride switchstance. Bindings positioned so your toes and heels sit right over the edges? Check. Having your boots centered side-to-side gives you balance and leverage. Stance centered along the length of your board? Check. Shifted back is nice for freeriding, but will mess up your balance in the pipe. Finally, stance width Okay? Too narrow will toss you over the nose and tail, so you want to go wide. Then again, too wide feels awkward and slows rotation. Strike a balance for stability and spin. Oh ya, one more thing: Edges de-tuned? Check. Sharp edges between the bindings are good; sharp edges at the tip and tail are scary. Edge catch to face smack. Ouch.

Okay, all set. You buckle in, stretch your legs, and gaze down the pipe. It's early yet, so there are no big "highways" or kinks visible in either of its walls. In fact most of the regulars are still fast asleep, so you've basically got the place to yourself. Good. For the moment you can take it super s-l-o-w-l-y, without the distractions or pressure of traffic.

Time for some warm-up runs. You stand up and drop in, heading for the backside wall first. Remember to keep the speed down—your only goal at first is to get a feel for it. You take the first hit nice and easy, going up the wall on your heelside edge, pulling the board around 180 degrees as you start to stall, and then dropping back in on your toeside edge. This part of riding the pipe is always the same: You take off and land on your uphill edge. Next you cross the *flat bottom*, heading for the frontside wall. Up on your toeside, nice clean 180, drop back in on your heelside.

As you wait for your muscles to coordinate with your brain, you wind up sliding down the wall without changing edges on your first few hits. As you hike back up for another run, you think *quick switch*. As you ride up the wall, you want to feel yourself start to stall, then quickly switch edges by turning back into the pipe with your body. Heading fairly straight at the wall, having enough speed but not too much, and keeping your midsection firm will all make the 180 easier. It also helps to spot your landing, and to lead the whole motion with your hands.

Eventually you get a nice rhythm going, and it's time to crank it up a notch. You want to get *above the lip* on every hit, so you add juice a little at a time and build up to it. The line with the frontside hit first feels most comfortable, so you add more speed going into the first hit. You push down into your board through the transition, pumping the wall, and spot the lip. When you hit it

Barrett Christy took the U.S. Snowboard scene by storm, winning so many contests in her first two years on tour that the snowboard community granted her a discretionary slot on the '98 Olympic team. Known as much for her positive attitude and sense of humor as for "going really big," Barrett's first signature model board from Gnu featured flying pigs.

Dorion Vidal, '98 U.S. Open, Stratton, Vermont.

you jump, extending first and then tucking your legs up close to your body as you stall in midair. As you drop back in, you turn, pointing the nose of your board back into the pipe and looking for your landing.

Pretty soon you're an adrenaline slave, hiking way past pooped in search of bigger air and new tricks. As you get more air, it's actually easier to hold it all together if you *grab*. First you grab your toeside edge off that first frontside hit because your hand is already there and so is your board. Don't get too psyched and freak though; you don't want to miss the landing. Once you nail it, you do the same grab off a backside hit until you can stick that one, too.

From there it all flows pretty naturally. You switch hands, so you can grab both sides of your board on either wall of the pipe. Then you grab further back toward the tail and push your front leg out until you can "bone" it. Next you might want to reach around and grab an edge with your opposite hand, or reach way back and grab the tail of your board. Go for whatever feels good, 'cuz that's what makes your style.

By lunchtime you're worked so you empty your pack, swapping snacks and insights with your pals. You find someone whose opinion you trust and listen, watching the big dogs for tips. Somebody's even got a video camera so you get all fired up again and trade off, taking runs and taping each other.

Eventually your second wind gives way to a third, which just gives way. Before you get too tired and really smack, you head home. Time for a feast, a hot tub, a nap. Who knows, you might even dream up a new trick for tomorrow. . . .

RESOURCE DIRECTORY: A WHOLE NEW KIND OF GIRLY ENTERTAINMENT

Rider: Tricia Byrnes

CAMPS AND INSTRUCTIONAL PROGRAMS FOR WOMEN

Delaney Adult Snowboard Camps
All-women's and mixed sessions, taught by glam brothers Kevin and Brian Delaney
Vail, CO
Phone 800-743-3790

High Cascade Snowboard Camp
Limited adult-only summer camp sessions at Mt. Hood, OR
Phone 800-334-4272
www.highcascade.com

Operation NBD
Women's instructional weekends
On Edge Girl's Board Shop
22311 Brookhurst Street
Huntington Beach, CA
Phone 714-965-9283

Wild Women Snowboard Camps
P.O. Box 10995
Jackson, WY
Phone 1-877-SHE-RIPS

Women On Board
Whitetail, PA
Phone 717-328-9400
email: Montane@juno.com

Women Only Snowboard Camps
Bridge Street Marketplace
P.O. Box 766
Waitsfield, VT 05673
Phone 800-552-5065, 800-451-4574
www.snowevents.com

EVENTS

Not listed, but worthwhile are early-season on-snow equipment demos. Dates
and locations for these vary, so check the fall snowboard magazines for manufacturer demo tour schedules. Also contact your destination resort, any local snowboard shops, and the manufacturer 800 numbers listed below.

Boarding for Breast Cancer
Annual spring fundraiser at Lake Tahoe, CA's Sierra-at-Tahoe resort
Fuse Sports Marketing
431 Pine Street
Burlington, VT 05401
Phone 802-864-7123
email: fuse@together.net

Fresh Session
Early-season girl snowboarder powwow at Sugarbush, VT
Women Only Snowboard Camps
Phone 800-552-5065, 800-451-4574

U.S. Open
The biggest, baddest, longest-running

*annual contest in snowboarding. Late
March, Stratton, VT.*
Burton Snowboards
80 Industrial Parkway
Burlington, VT 05401
Phone 800-881-3138
www.burton.com

**World Cup and U.S. Snowboard
  Tours**
*Catch a contest and see the pros
in action*
c/o U.S. Snowboarding
P.O. Box 100
Park City, UT 84060
Phone 801-647-2626
www.ussnowboard.com

MAGAZINES

**Couloir, The
  Backcountry Snowboard
  & Ski Magazine**
P.O. Box 2349
Truckee, CA 96160
Phone 530-582-1884
www.couloir-mag.com

**Fresh and Tasty Women's
  Snowboarding**
*Note: On 8/31/98, we learned that this
popular magazine had suspended publication. We list it as a resource hoping
that publication resumes—either in
print, online, or both. The website has
many links to women and snowboarding.*
100 Spring Street
Cambridge, MA 02141
www.freshandtasty.com.

Mountainfreak
P.O. Box 4149
Telluride, CO 81435
Phone 970-728-9731
www.mountainfreak.com

Mountain Sport & Living
810 Seventh Avenue
New York, NY 10019
Phone 800-333-2299
www.MountainZone.com/MSL
(formerly *Snow Country*)

Snowboarder Magazine
33046 Calle Aviador

San Juan Capistrano, CA 92675
P.O. Box 1028
Dana Point, CA 92629
Phone 714-496-5922
www.snowboardermag.com

Snowboard Life Magazine
353 Airport Road
Oceanside, CA 92054-1203
Phone 760-722-7777

Snowboarding Online
www.solsnowboarding.com

Transworld Snowboarding Magazine
353 Airport Road
Oceanside, CA 92054-1203
Phone 760-722-7777

MANUFACTURERS

*Please note that this is not a compre-
hensive list, but only those vendors
mentioned in earlier chapters. Also
listed are a few worthy candidates we
just couldn't fit elsewhere.*

Airwalk
Hardgoods, softgoods and accessories
Phone 800-AIRWALK
www.airwalk.com

Arnette Optical
900 Calle Negocio
San Clemente, CA 92673
Phone 800-742-8530

**Avalanche Snowboards/
  A Sport**
991 Tyler Street, Bldg. 200
Benicia, CA 94510
Phone 800-222-8820

Betty Rides Clothing
130 S.E. 53rd Ave.
Portland, OR 97215
Phone 503-235-8770
email: betty@europa.com

**Boeri Helmets-MPH Associates,
  Inc.**
Building 52, 61 Endicott Street
P.O. Box 567
Norwood, MA 02062
Phone 781-555-9933

Bonfire Clothing
525 SE 11th Avenue
Portland, OR 97214
Phone 503-236-3473

Burton Snowboards
Hardgoods, softgoods, accessories
80 Industrial Parkway
Burlington, VT 05401
Phone 800-881-3138

Clif Bar/Kali's Sport Naturals
1610 5th Street
Berkeley, CA 94710
Phone 510-558-7855
www.clifbar.com

Cold As Ice Clothing
Women's snowboard clothing
234 E. 17th Street, Suite 116
Costa Mesa, CA 92627
Phone 949-642-6790

**Columbia Sportswear/Convert
  Snowboard Apparel**
P.O. Box 83239
Portland, OR 97283-0239
Phone 800-547-8066
www.columbia.com

Crash Pads
Hillsboro, OR
Phone 503-640-2669

Da Kine
All sorts of accessories
408 Columbia Street
Suite 300
Hood River, OR 97031
Phone 541-386-3166
www.dakine.com

Deep
Women's snowboard clothing
1218 West Yarnell Drive
Larkspur, CO 80118
Phone 719-481-4513

**Gnu Snowboards/Mervin
  Manufacturing**
Hardgoods
2600 West Commodore Way
Seattle, WA 98199
Phone 206-270-9792
www.mervin.com

Goddess Snowboards
1916 Spice Tree Lane, SE
Salem, OR 97306
Phone 503-399-7452

Grabber Warmers
Disposable hand and boot warmers
4600 Danvers Drive SE
Grand Rapids, MI 49512
Phone 800-423-1233

K2 Snowboards
19215 Vashon Highway SW
Vashon Island, WA 98070
Phone 800-972-4038
www.k2sports.com

Morrow Snowboards/Westbeach
   Clothing
2600 Pringle Road SE
P.O. Box 12606
Salem, OR 97309
Phone 503-375-9300
www.morrowsnowboards.com

Motorola
2-way radios
Phone 800-353-2729
www.arsradio.com

N Boots/Northwave North
   America
7735 178th Place NE
Suite B
Redmond, WA 98053
www.northwave.com

Nidecker Snowboards
1 Steele Street
Burlington, VT 05401
Phone 888-693-8789
www.nidecker.ch

Nikwax Waterproofing Systems
P.O. Box 1572
Everett, WA 98206
Phone 800-335-0260

Numb
Padded long underwear and tops
18 Haven Avenue
Suite 203
Port Washington, NY 11050
Phone 516-767-7761
Phone 800-932-6862

Oakley Eyewear
714-951-0991

Patagonia Mail Order, Inc.
Also available in zillions of stores
8550 White Fir Street
P.O. Box 32050
Reno, Nevada 89533-2050
Phone 800-638-6464
www.patagonia.com

Peregrine Outfitters
Outdoor accessories and books
P.O. Box 1500
105 S. Brownell Road
Williston, VT 05495
Phone 800-222-3088

Pro-Tec
Helmets and pads
111 Pier Avenue
Suite 100
Hermosa Beach, CA 90254
Phone 800-338-6068

Raichle Molitor USA, Inc.
Boots
Geneva Road
Brewster, NY 10509
Phone 914-279-5121

Ride Snowboards
8160 304th Avenue SE
Preston, WA 98050
Phone 425-222-6015

Root 100
*Ginseng chew, in flavors you'd never
imagine—tangerine, apple, pepper-
mint, cinnamon, ginger, and original.*
Vermont Ginseng Products
P.O. Box 6
Waterbury, VT 05676
Phone 800-270-0007
email: vtginseng@aol.com
www.root100.com

Rossignol
Phone 802-863-2511

Roxy/Quiksilver Clothing
5600 Argosy Circle
Building 100
Huntington Beach, CA 92649
Phone 714-645-1395

Salomon North America
Hardgoods
400 East Main Street
Georgetown, MA 01833
Phone 800-225-6850

Sierra Designs
Clothing
1255 Powell Street
Emeryville, CA 94608
Phone 510-450-9555

Sims Snowboards
Thrashers Corner
22105 23rd Drive SE
Mill Creek, WA 98021
Phone 425-951-2700

Smith Sport Optics
Phone 800-459-4903
www.smithsport.com

Superfeet
Aftermarket footbeds
1419 Whitehorn Street
Ferndale, WA 98248
Phone 800-634-6618

Test Pilot
Tools, locks and other accessories
716 Highway 10
Suite 128
Minneapolis, MN 55434
Phone 800-780-4911

Title 9 Sports
*Mail-order sports bras and women's
   clothing*
5743 Landregan Street
Emeryville, CA 94608
Phone 510-653-9949

Turtle Fur Company
*Makers of the original super-deluxe
   fleece neckwarmers*
P.O. Box 1010
Lamoille Industrial Park
Morrisville, VT 05661-1010
Phone 800-52-NECKS

Vans Shoes/Switch Manufacturing
*Vans=soft boots; Switch=step-in boots
   and bindings*
15700 Shoemaker Avenue
Sante Fe Springs, CA 90670

Phone 800-826-7800
www.vans.com

Wave Rave Clothing
Including hard-to-find women's
* Gore-Tex outerwear*
2340 West 2nd Avenue
Denver, CO 80223
Phone 888-442-3080

RESORT INFORMATION

Please note this is by no means a comprehensive list. These are just a few of the resorts known for attracting snowboarders. Some resorts have separate lines for information and reservations, so please note that (I) = information phone number and (R) = reservations phone number.

UNITED STATES

CALIFORNIA
Bear Mountain
Phone 909-585-2519

Mammoth Mountain
Phone (I) 888-462-6668
Phone (R) 888-466-2666
www.mammoth-mtn.com

Sierra at Tahoe
Phone 530-659-7453

Snow Summit
Phone 909-866-5766

Squaw Valley
Phone 800-545-4350

COLORADO
Arapahoe Basin
Phone 970-468-0718
www.arapahoebasin.com

Beaver Creek
Phone 800-944-4973
www.snow.com

Breckenridge
Phone (I) 800-789-7669
Phone (R) 800-221-1091
www.snow.com

Copper Mountain
Phone 800-458-8386
www.ski-copper.com

Crested Butte
Phone 800-544-8448
www.crestedbutteresort.com

Purgatory/Durango
Phone 800-525-0892
www.ski-purg.com

Telluride
Phone 888-355-8743
www.telski.com

Vail
Phone 800-404-3535
www.snow.com

Wolf Creek
Phone 970-264-5639
www.wolfcreekski.com

MAINE
Sugarloaf
Phone 800-843-5623
www.sugarloaf.com

Sunday River
Phone 800-543-2754
www.sundayriver.com

MONTANA
Big Mountain
Phone (I) 406-862-2900
Phone (R) 800-858-5439
www.bigmtn.com

Big Sky
Phone 800-548-4486
www.bigskyresort.com

Red Lodge
Phone 800-444-8977
www.montana.net/rlmresort

NEW HAMPSHIRE
Waterville Valley
Phone 800-468-2553
www.waterville.com

OREGON
Mt. Bachelor
Phone 541-382-7888
www.mtbachelor.com

Mt. Hood
Phone 503-272-3206
www.skibowl.com

UTAH
Brighton
Phone (I) 810-532-4731
Phone (R) 800-873-5512
www.skibrighton.com

Snowbird
Phone (I) 801-742-2222
Phone (R) 800-453-3000
www.snowbird.com

Solitude
Phone (I) 801-534-1400
Phone (R) 800-748-4754
www.skisolitude.com

VERMONT
Jay Peak
Phone 800-451-4449
www.jaypeakresort.com

Killington
Phone (I) 802-422-6200
Phone (R) 800-621-6867
www.killington.com

Mount Snow
Phone (I) 800-245-SNOW
Phone (R) 800-451-4211
www.mountsnow.com

Stowe
Phone (I) 802-253-3000
Phone (R) 800-253-4754
www.stowe.com

Stratton
Phone 802-297-2200

Sugarbush
Phone 800-537-8427
www.sugarbush.com

WASHINGTON

Mt. Baker
Phone 360-734-6711
www.mtbakerskiarea.com

WYOMING

Grand Targhee
Phone 800-827-4433
www.grandtarghee.com

Jackson Hole
Phone 800-443-6931
www.jacksonhole.com/ski

CANADA

ALBERTA

Banff/Lake Louise
Phone (I) 1-800-258-SNOW
Phone (R) 403-256-0473
www.skilouise.com

BRITISH COLUMBIA

Blackcomb
Phone 800-944-7853
www.whistler-blackcomb.com

Whistler
Phone 800-944-7853
www.whistler-resort.com

QUEBEC

Mont St. Anne
Phone 418-827-4561
www.mont-sainte-anne.com

Mont Tremblant
Phone 800-567-6760
www.tremblant.com

SHOP INFORMATION

There are way too many shops to list here. To find the snowboard- and female-friendliest shop(s) near you,

- Ask a friendly neighborhood snowboarder.
- Check one of the snowboard magazines listed above for a retail directory that lists shops by region.

- Call the 800 number for a manufacturer you're interested in and ask for a dealer near you.

TRADE ASSOCIATION

For general information and links all over the snow industry, visit the website for the snowboard industry trade association:

SnowSports Industries America (SIA)
8377-B Greensboro Drive
McLean, VA 22102-3587
Phone 703-556-9020
www.snowlink.com

VIDEOS

Room and Board/J2 Productions
All-girl snowboard vids and more
P.O. Box 513
Avon, CO 81620
Phone 970-827-4117
email: rbj2@colorado.net

WEATHER INFORMATION

For road conditions, forecasts and snow reports for your favorite resorts:

- Check the Weather Channel (great for your local forecast, but you may have to wait to see it).

- Get one of those nifty little portable weather radios (nothin' but your regional weather, all day long, at the touch of a button. Plus they cost maybe $20 at your favorite electronics store).

- Check the snow report at your destination resort. (Great for very specific information about snowfall, trails and grooming, but keep in mind these reports are provided by the resorts marketeers. Usually a recording available by phone, or you can sign up to have a written report emailed to you.)

- Finally for all you web junkies, (as if you didn't know already), is the National Weather Service's home page: HYPER-LINK http://www.nws.fsu.edu (Great if you're planning to travel. Flip through and find snow reports, forecasts and road conditions for almost any location).

WOMEN'S EQUIPMENT INFORMATION

Technical advice, chat, product updates and testing reports on all the latest women's gear. Write for stickers and information.

Tech Betty* Snowboarding
P.O. Box 712
Stowe, VT 05672
coming soon: www.techbetty.com

WOMEN'S ETC.

Ride Like A Girl™
Stickers and t-shirts
Team Betty*
P.O. Box 744
Wellfleet, MA 02667
800-93-BETTY

*Who's Betty? Betty used to be a derogatory nickname for a girl snowboarder, as in, "Who's that?," "Oh, some betty." Then Ali Napolitano and her friend Kristen turned it around with Team Betty. Their original t-shirts read: "My boyfriend told me if I go snowboarding one more time it's over" on the front. The back read: "See ya." They sell stickers that say it all with a simple phrase: Ride Like A Girl.™